A NEW PERSPECTIVE ON THE BOOK OF JOB

A New Perspective on the Book of Job

By Winson Elgersma
B.A., B.D., LL.B.

A New Perspective on the Book of Job

© Winson Elgersma 2018

All rights reserved. Without limiting the rights under copyright reserved above, no part of this publication may be reproduced, stored in a retrieval system, or transmitted, in any form or by any means (electronic, mechanical, photocopying, recording or otherwise), without the prior written permission of the copyright owner of this book.

Published by
Lighthouse Christian Publishing
SAN 257-4330
5531 Dufferin Drive
Savage, Minnesota, 55378
United States of America

www.lighthousechristianpublishing.com

TABLE OF CONTENTS

Acknowledgments

Introduction

PART ONE:

The Book of Job Opened

Chapter 1: The Key Question

Chapter 2: The Great Debate – Round One

Chapter 3: The Great Debate – Round Two

Chapter 4: The Great Debate – Round Three

Chapter 5: Analyzing the Debate

Chapter 6: God's Response

Chapter 7: Epilogue

Chapter 8: Post Script

PART TWO:

The Book of Job Applied

Chapter 9: The Changing Concept of Human Nature

Chapter 10: The Biblical Concept of Human Nature

End Notes

A Note to the Reader

About the Author

ACKNOWLEDGMENTS

I wish to acknowledge the following people who helped me with this undertaking. Because writing requires commitment, and thinking requires concentration, I very much appreciated the time and space that my wife, Joyce, gave me. She was also prepared to listen to "read backs" and to offer helpful suggestions. Our eldest son, Delbert, would often take time from his busy legal practice to read portions of the book, and to offer advice as to syntax and wording. When dealing with the section on suffering, our son, Vincent, a physician, brought new perspectives. Our daughter Laura, an award-winning teacher, consistently gave me the psychological impetus to continue. Questions from Chad, an anesthesiologist, and the youngest of our children, were always a reminder that more needed to be done. Thanks also to Warren Elgersma, an instructor at Red Deer College, for his immediate willingness to review the manuscript. My good friend, Jake Masselink, was one of the first to read the manuscript and his encouragement, especially early on, was invaluable. John Zylstra (now retired) brought his experience as a publisher to bear on this book and his counsel was priceless. Dave De Haan, a fellow classmate and pastor, critiqued the book and his recommendations were helpful. Rita Vandenberg would frequently inquire about the book, and the information gained from her during our discussions was thought provoking. Dick Van Veldhuisen's interest in the subject matter was also encouraging.

INTRODUCTION

This book, *A New Perspective on the Book of Job*, seeks to help us understand and appreciate the *Book of Job*, that for reasons provided in Chapter 1, is often difficult to understand. It consists of ten chapters, and is written from the point of view of Eliphaz, one of the participants in the debate.

Chapter 1 identifies the parties involved, and discloses why the debaters, (all friends) eventually engaged in such an acrimonious dispute that, but for God's intervention, would have cost them their friendship. The dispute arose from the effort of three friends to explain why Job was suffering so intensely. They alleged that his suffering arose as punishment for sins that inevitably flowed from his inherently sinful human nature. Job rejected their allegation, and contended that his tribulations could not have arisen from his sinful nature because he was a righteous man.

Chapter 1 also provides the key question necessary to unlocking the message, namely; why did God, after the dispute was over, accuse the friends of slandering Him, i.e. God? This is all the more mystifying given that the friends (and even some subsequent commentators) thought that they were speaking highly of God.

Chapters 2-4 is an easy to read summary of the controversy, with Job on one side, and his three friends on the other. It furnishes the background and information essential to understanding God's reaction. There are many surprises that arise from the debate, but the greatest surprise, at least from the friends' point of view, occurred when God accused them of slander.

Chapter 5 is an analysis of the dispute, and fleshes out and discloses some of the subtleties of the arguments. The positions taken by the debaters are graphically portrayed through a comparative analysis. It also deals with the differing concepts of human nature held by the opposing parties.

Chapter 6 contains God's surprising response to the debate. Although it is directed at Job, it is intended to teach all of us something about human nature, the sovereignty of God, people's suffering, and the presence of evil in the world. The examples and illustrations, by which God chose to convey His message, are absolutely fascinating and compelling, although largely misunderstood.

Chapter 7 answers the question: why did God accuse the friends of slandering Him? It carefully analyses the sin of slander, and identifies those statements made by the friends that God found offensive.

Chapter 8 deals with the mysterious appearance of Elihu. It also sets out the various theories advanced by various writers and scholars as to why God was angry, and it identifies those statements that were false, but not slanderous.

Chapter 9 traces, reviews, and evaluates, various concepts of human nature from the time of Christ to the advent of Calvinism.

Chapter 10 sets out the Scriptural view of human nature, and applies the lessons learned from the *Book of Job*.

One of the reasons contributing to the difficulty in understanding the *Book of Job*, are the significant differences in various translations. When referring to these differing translations, I will use the following abbreviations.

NIV – New International Version
NLT – New Living Translation
NASV – New American Standard Version
KJV – King James Version
HCSB – Holman Christian Standard Bible

PART ONE

THE BOOK OF JOB OPENED

CHAPTER 1

THE KEY QUESTION

Introduction

    My name is Eliphaz, and I was a friend of Job. One day I heard that he was suffering from a terrible disease, so I contacted Bildad and Zophar, two other friends, and we decided to visit him. The purpose was to express our sympathy, and to comfort him. We lived a significant distant from each other, so it took some time to organize the trip. We met where our roads converged, and thereafter we traveled together. I came from a city called Teman, which was akin to a university town, and which was renowned for its higher learning.[1] My two friends came from elsewhere, but we were all considered wise men. We were not only educated in religious matters, but also in history and in law.

My Friend Job
    When I last visited Job, he was a rich and prosperous man, with huge holdings in livestock, and a large number of servants to care for them. He lived in Uz, an area east of the Jordon River, and was known as the greatest man among all the people of the east.
    He had ten children, seven sons and three daughters, whom he loved very much. He would often speak of them with great fondness, and when any of them approached him, his smile could not be suppressed.

The children's respect and admiration for their father was obvious in the way they spoke to him. I was struck by their desire to be near him, and as a result he was seldom alone. His children regularly sought his advice.

In the background, there were always a number of household servants who responded immediately when summoned by Job. He spoke to them with a gentle, non-condescending voice, and his instructions were clear and concise.

He had a large and beautiful home surrounded by the homes of his married children. Beyond the family homes were the servants' quarters. All the pathways seemed to converge on Job's house, and all were well worn.

In our time the village square was the place where people often gathered to discuss current affairs, or to conduct business. The arguments that ensued were often heated, and Job was frequently called upon to be the peacemaker. It was also the place for the exchange of ideas. Political and philosophical theories were advanced and debated. Job enjoyed participating in these debates, and he regularly distinguished himself through his thoughtful presentations.

In addition to his responsibilities as a husband, father, teacher, employer, businessman, and peacemaker, Job was also a de facto judge. He was exceptionally well educated, and had a deserved reputation as a wise, and clear thinking arbiter. He had the gift of discernment, and an unshakeable sense of fairness. As a result, people would seek him out to settle their disputes, and to ask his advice.

From time to time he would take his seat in the public square, and hear the complaints of the people. Because of his status in the community, he was expected to take the most prominent seat. If the seat were occupied before his arrival, the occupant would immediately relinquish it.

The hearings were outside and all were oral. They were mostly unorganized, in that no one prioritized the sequence.

People would simply line up, and approach him when their time came. Job had no advance notice of what was coming. There were no lawyers, although people were permitted to speak on behalf of others.

Job was particularly attentive to the concerns of the poor, the widows, and the disabled. He believed in the judicial principle of restitution, and where possible required the wrongdoers to make right the wrong they had caused. If restitution were not possible, he would often provide relief from his own resources. When questioning the litigants, he insisted on the truth, and was merciless to those who attempted to deceive him. In describing his quest for the truth, Job told us: "the cause which I knew not, I searched out."[2]

When Job took the time to reflect, people waited expectantly. His decisions were always well reasoned, and when rendered the combatants were silent. There was nothing more to say.

Those who knew him well, as I did, considered him a man of upright character and blameless conduct. As a man of character, he was honest, faithful, and sincere. He was interested in the lives of his friends, and his inquiries as to their welfare, were always genuine. He was intellectually curious, and actively solicited the thoughts of others. He respected their opinions, and responded accordingly. I was very fond of him. He was a man of integrity, and I considered myself fortunate to have him as a friend.

Job's Suffering

When Bildad, Zophar, and I came near to Job's house, we saw a badly disfigured person sitting on a mound of ashes. He looked terrible. From the top of his head to the soles of his feet he had something that looked like boils. They oozed with pus. He was dirty and his beard was untrimmed. His clothing was stained with vomit, and his body reeked. We wanted to avoid this wretch, but to reach Job's house we had to pass closely by.

It was only then that we realized that this was Job. We were shocked. He was obviously suffering terribly and we began to weep. We tore our clothes, and sprinkled dust on our heads to demonstrate our sadness, and our solidarity with him. I wanted to embrace him, but because of his repulsive condition, I was unable to do so.

He attempted to acknowledge our presence, but all we heard were sighs, groans, and other expressions of pain. The groans came from deep within him, and he occasionally cried out. He finally gave up trying to speak, and he wept uncontrollably.

Job's house, if you could call it that, was directly behind him. It was a dilapidated heap, unfit for human habitation: a hovel that at some point would need to be disinfected.[3]

As was the practice in our culture, the very sick were often kept in a separate area of the house, with a few servants to care for them. It soon became apparent that, although there were a few servants present, none would attend to him. From time to time he would call for one, especially at night, but no one ever responded.[4]

The only person who would come near him was his wife, who brought him his food. He would drink a little, but his food was generally untouched. When he did eat something, his body rejected it in the form of vomit or diarrhea.[5]

When we first arrived he seemed embarrassed by his appearance, but over time he didn't even try to hide his body's failings. He appeared to have no pride, and no self-esteem left.

He spent much of his time sitting or lying outside in the shade. He slept very little, and at night we took turns staying up with him. He said nothing, but his groans said everything. Occasionally the pain was so severe that beads of sweat would break out through the scabs. He had suffered this way for months. I had some knowledge of diseases, but this was unlike anything I had seen before. I would often find myself weeping for my friend. I had known him as strong, confident and proud, and now I saw him as weak, emaciated, and pathetic.

His physical pain was self evident, but only he knew the extent of his emotional pain. Almost everyday he would whisper the name of one or more of his children, and then he would simply sob – long, deep and intense sobs – the likes of which I had never heard before.

Contributing to his emotional pain was the loss of his status in the community. Many found his physical appearance revolting, and they mocked him. Those whom he had previously benefitted, now turned against him. Some sang songs of derision, while others spit in his face. He saw their hostility, and he felt exposed and unsafe.

His faith brought little solace, because he believed that God had deserted him. The depth of his disappointment could not be measured. He had hoped for good, but evil came instead. He had lived a life of obedience, because he feared the punishment of God. Now he was experiencing that which he had tried so hard to avoid. For months he had cried out: "why?" but God had not responded.

In our culture no one speaks to someone who is obviously suffering so intensely, until he/she speaks first. As a result, we sat on the ground with him for seven days during which time no one said a word. But that did not stop us from wondering what had he done to deserve this? We knew him to be a man of upright character and blameless conduct, but he was clearly being punished for something. He must be harboring some horrific hidden sins in his heart, or perhaps, he had even committed some odious overt sins of which we were unaware. We believed that in order to be restored to his former state, it would be important for him to acknowledge his sins, whether hidden or overt.

The Dispute

Eventually Job spoke. He alleged that God was to blame for his severe suffering. This led to a long debate as to the cause of his tribulations. In short, we believed that all people are born evil, vile and corrupt. It was impossible for anyone, including Job, not to have sinned. Therefore, when God punished him, he had only himself to blame.

When Job continued to insist that he had not sinned, we were surprised. However, this surprise was nothing compared to the surprise we received when the debate was over, and God accused us of slander. At first we thought that God had accused us of slandering Job. After all, we had often spoken disparagingly about him. But no, He accused us of slandering Him, i.e. God. He then required us to atone for our sin of slander by way of a sacrifice. What made matters worse; He also required that we approach Job (the man we had accused of hypocrisy) and ask him to pray for us. God's indictment, and our humiliation were recorded in perpetuity for all generations to see.

> *After the Lord had said these things to Job, He said to Eliphaz the Temanite, "I am angry with you and your two friends, because you have not spoken of <u>me</u> what is right, as my servant Job has. So now take seven bulls and seven rams and go to my servant Job and sacrifice a burnt offering for yourselves. My servant Job will pray for you, and I will accept his prayer and not deal with you according to your folly. You have not spoken of <u>me</u> what is right as my servant Job has."*[6]

At first we were dumbfounded. We were simply encouraging Job to confess his sins so God would no longer punish him. But Job had insisted that God was punishing a righteous man, which was preposterous. God would never do that. We thought that we were defending God.

We have since learned that what we said did indeed slander Him, but that revelation did not come easily. At first my friends and I struggled to identify those specific statements that so offended God. Each of us had our own ideas, but ultimately we came to a consensus, and acknowledged that what we said was wrong.

As was the case with us, I note that throughout the ages, even Biblical scholars struggled to find the answer as to why God was angry. There are many competing theories and in chapter 8, I will show what they are. Some do not even attempt an explanation.

But how can one claim to understand the *Book of Job* if our offensive statements cannot be identified? God's entire lesson would have been wasted on us, if we had not understood how we had offended Him. It is the key to understanding the book.

I should explain that I died thousands of years ago, and after I entered the afterlife, I was given the gift of transcendence. This enables me to move backwards and forwards in time, and as a result I am able to review and evaluate all historical and current information, events, and publications, concerning our dispute with Job.

About the Book of Job

The *Book of Job* is the oldest book in the Bible. I do not know who authored the book, but because it so accurately represents what was said during the debate, I suspect it may have been Job, who wrote it after my death.

The Book is not long, and I believe you will agree that it is one of the most fascinating books in the *Bible*. Based on the various translations and interpretations, it is my belief that of all the Biblical books, it is the most misunderstood. The primary subject matter is not suffering, punishment, perseverance or faith as many people believe. Rather, at its core, it is a book that examines the extent of the goodness, or sinfulness, of human nature. Or to express it another way, it is a book that inquires into a person's capacity to overcome their sinful nature. It is a book of enormous depth that diminishes the dread of death, provides solace for those who suffer, and hope for those burdened with guilt.

I acknowledge that on first reading the book is difficult to understand. It employs a number of literary tools such as rhetorical questions, references to oriental mythologies, obscure metaphors, sarcasm, exaggeration and innuendo. Also, so as to diminish the hurt of our accusations, we would often speak as if we were describing or criticizing a third person, when in fact, we were addressing each other. Further, except for the prologue and the epilogue, the book is written as a poem. As such, thoughts are compressed and words are chosen to meet the requirements of poetry.

The book consists of five parts:
1. The Prologue – chapters 1 and 2
2. The great debate – chapters 3—31
3. A speech attributed to Elihu – chapters 32—37
4. God's response – chapters 38—41 and
5. The Epilogue – chapter 42.

In my study of law, I learned that the most fundamental rule of interpretation is to allow a document (including a book) to speak for itself, and not to read into it any preconceived notions. However, if a book is to speak, it must be conveyed in a language that the reader understands. Consequently, what follows in the next three chapters of this book, is a simplified, abbreviated, and easy to read summary of the debate, with Job on one side, and my friends and I on the other. I have made every effort to accurately reflect the spirit and intent of each speaker's argument. Throughout the debate some notes and commentary will be provided (in brackets) to demonstrate how the arguments are developing, or to provide clarity.

Because I wish the book to speak for itself, I have not included quotes from scholars or commentaries except where

necessary. Still, because the book is difficult to understand, I have provided the following assistance.
1. In those circumstances where we spoke as if we were addressing a third party, when in fact our message was meant for Job, the pretense is discarded and the dialogue directed to the intended recipient. Unfortunately for us, it then becomes clear how cruel our words were, and I now deeply regret them.
2. Much is said by way of inference or innuendo. So as to give clarity to the arguments, I have occasionally expressed what the inference or innuendo was intended to convey.

The debate consists of three rounds. In each round we take turns trying to explain to Job why he was suffering so intensely. We were insistent that he was being punished with suffering, because his human nature was so sinful that he must have sinned. But Job insisted that he was a righteous man, and although he believed that his suffering came from the hand of God, he was certain that it was not because of any sin arising from his human nature.

Unfortunately, our initial desire to express our sympathy, and to comfort him, quickly morphed into a desire to correct him. But God was not angry with us because of our change of attitude toward Job. Rather, He was offended by what we said or implied about Him. So once again the question surfaces: what did we say about God, whether directly or by implication, that so angered Him?

Prologue (Job 1; 2)

The *Book of Job* begins by describing Job's happy circumstances prior to his tribulations. It then states: "One day the angels came to present themselves before the Lord, and Satan also came with them."[7] It was at that time that God asked him, "Have you considered my servant Job? ... He is blameless as well as upright, a man who fears God and shuns evil."[8]

Satan responded by saying: of course he is, but that is because you have enticed him through your many blessings, to be a man of upright character and blameless conduct. But I know how to make him sin. "If you reach out and take away everything he has, he will surely curse you to your face."[9]

So God gave Satan permission to destroy everything that Job had. First a marauding tribe came and stole his oxen and donkeys, and killed the servants that worked with them. Then lightning struck, and burned the sheep and other servants. Thereafter, raiding parties stole the camels and killed the remaining hired hands. Finally, Job's ten children were killed when a wind blew their house down. Job, of course, did not know it was the devil's doing. Despite his belief that God had caused his enormous and catastrophic loss, Job did not curse Him as Satan said he would.

The next time God and Satan met, God pointed out that despite what happened to him, Job continued to be a blameless and upright man, who revered God, and shunned evil. In addition God said: "and he maintains his integrity."[10] That is to say: he remained honest, upright and faithful to his beliefs.

Consequently, Satan upped the anti. "If you reach out, and take away his health, he will surely curse you to your face."[11] God again gave permission, and Satan afflicted Job with extremely painful and unsightly conditions that affected his entire body, from the soles of his feet to the top of his head. It got to the point where Job was found outside, sitting on a mound of ashes, scraping his purulent skin with a piece of broken pottery. Finally, Job's wife said to him, "Are you still holding on to your beliefs? Curse God and die."[12] As we will see, Job very much wanted to die, but he did not curse God, even though he was certain that it was God who was causing him to suffer.

Although Job did not curse God for the constant pain and severe suffering that he thought came from the hand of God, he did become bitter. Throughout his life he had sought to please God, and had always treated other people accordingly. As a result he expected a healthy and prosperous life surrounded by family, but instead, he believed that God had destroyed his family and allotted him unspeakable pain and distress. He felt that God had wronged him, and he was not reluctant to express his bitterness and disappointment.

[It should be noted that in the Jewish tradition, Satan is not a person, but a title representing a function. He is described as "The Satan," meaning "The Prosecutor." It was his duty to go to and fro on the earth, and to seek out and prosecute the wrongdoers. He is not a fallen angel, as portrayed in the Christian tradition, but a high ranking and respected angel. Hence, when the angels came to present themselves before the Lord, it was wholly appropriate that he be present.[13]]

CHAPTER 2

THE GREAT DEBATE: ROUND 1

Job [Eventually Job spoke. I am sure he assumed it would be a sympathetic, and comforting conversation among close friends with whom he could speak and complain freely.]
I wish I had never been born, but given that I was born, I wish I had died at birth. Then at least I could find some rest and relief. In fact, I wish that the date of my birth had never existed, because it ultimately brought me nothing but pain and sorrow. If anyone wants to curse a day, let him call on the Leviathan, and curse that day. My earnest desire is to die. (Job then asks the following four questions.)
1. Why did I not perish at birth, and die as I came out of the womb? Then at least, I would be at rest with kings and people of wealth.
2. Why was I not a stillborn child? In death the wicked cease from trouble, and the weary are at rest. Prisoners do not hear the voice of their oppressors, and servants are free from their masters.
3. Why is light given to those in misery, and life to those who are bitter: who long for death as if it were a treasure, and rejoice when they find the grave?
4. Why is life given to those who have no future, and whom God has hedged in with suffering? I sigh from my pain and depression, and groans pour out from me like water. That which I feared most, I now experience: what I dreaded most, has now come true. I have no peace, no quietness, and no rest. Only suffering comes. (Chapter 3)
(The debate, beginning with Job's speech, was written as a poem. Throughout the poem the author often reiterates the same question, or repeats the same thing, using different

words. Job's questions illustrate this point. The first two express his desire never to have been born. The next two express his bewilderment as to why God would give life to those who cannot live it without bitterness or suffering.)

Eliphaz [Because I was the eldest, I was the first to respond. Job was my friend, but his questions revealed an inappropriate contempt for things regarded as sacred. The last question was especially offensive. In effect the question was: why would God give a person life in circumstances where He then makes it impossible for that person to enjoy that life? It is obvious from the context however, that this was not merely a theoretical question. He is in fact, alleging that God is responsible for depriving him of the capacity to enjoy life. It was important that I point out to him that he was blaming God for his dreadful circumstances when in fact, it was his own sins that brought this about.]

I know what I have to say may hurt you, but it must be said. In the past, you have encouraged, strengthened and supported many people in distress, but now you are discouraged and dismayed. Does not your pious character give you confidence, or your blameless ways hope? Who being blameless ever suffered like you? Or who being upright was ever devastated like you? As I have observed, evil comes to those who are evil, and trouble comes to troublemakers; and God destroys them all in anger.

You were a great lion, but your roar and growl are no more. You are perishing, because you can no longer make a living, and the teeth of the young lions are broken. As a result, your children were unable to defend themselves and like the scattered cubs of the lioness, they are gone.

Through a vision, I received a word that I must convey to you. As I think of it, fear and trembling seize me, and my bones shake. The word is: can a mortal be innocent before God? Can anyone be pure before the Creator? Surely, if the angels are imperfect; how much more imperfect are those who live in a body of clay, who will return to the dust, and who are crushed more easily than a moth? They are alive in the morning, but dead by evening, gone forever without a trace. And when they die, does not the excellence that is within them also perish?

Call if you will, but who will answer you? To which of the holy ones will you turn?

Anger kills fools, and envy destroys the simple. I myself have seen foolishness taking root in you, and I immediately cursed its dwelling. Your children became unsafe, and eventually they were sentenced without a defender. In addition, your harvest is stolen and your wealth is lost.

[The above paragraph is an example where, during the actual debate, I pretended to be speaking about fools generally, but the message was plainly intended for Job. In this summary, I have dropped the pretence, and directed my comments directly at Job. Also, when I said: "I immediately cursed its dwelling", what I meant was, I was trying to expunge his foolishness by cursing it, just like Job was trying to erase the day he was born by cursing it.]

Continuing – evil does not spring from the soil, neither does trouble sprout from the ground. It comes from within. All people are born wrongdoers, and as such they will do wrong – just as surely as sparks fly upwards from a fire.

If I were you, I would appeal to God, and commit my cause to Him. He can change your circumstances. He is a God of power and providence. He is the giver of all that which is good, but He punishes those who are evil. Do not resent His discipline. He injures, but He also heals. If you accept His correction, He will rescue you from your suffering, and you will be blessed and restored in every way. (Chapters 4,5)

[Job had, in effect, accused God of hedging him in with suffering, and I was eager to point out that his own sin was the cause of his dreadful condition. But I had a problem. I had no evidence of any sins that Job had actually committed.

Nonetheless there were some things that I strongly believed.
1. All human beings are born evil.
2. In fact, they are so evil, that they will inevitably sin.
3. It is God's will to punish those who sin.
4. God punishes the evildoer through suffering.
5. God will withdraw His punishment from those who acknowledge their wickedness and confess their sins, and they will be restored.

I then applied these religious beliefs to the circumstances at hand and my argument became:
1. You are suffering because you are being punished.
2. You are being punished because you were born an evildoer. Therefore, just as surely as sparks rise up from a fire, you have actually sinned.
3. If you confess your sins, God will rescue you from your suffering and restore you in every way.

I was well aware that Job had a reputation as a pious and righteous man, but I firmly believed that he could not be as righteous as he was reputed to be, and I told him so.
1. If you were righteous God would not be punishing you. But He is punishing you, and that proves that you are not righteous.
2. Righteousness and purity are qualities that belong exclusively to God. You are a man, and therefore you cannot be righteous.
3. In fact, by God's standards, even His angels are not pure, and you are less than an angel, therefore you cannot be pure.
4. You are a human being, and therefore, you were born evil.]

[**Job's** initial reaction was to attribute his impetuous comments to his anguish and misery, but the more he spoke the more despondent he seemed to become. Part of his despondency could probably be attributed to the weight of his unrelenting pain, but the greater part arose from my accusations, and his disappointment in my failure to support and comfort him.]

My anguish and misery cannot be weighed. They are too great to bear. No wonder that my words may have been impetuous, but God has caused me great suffering. Do I not have reason to complain? Does a wild donkey complain when it has grass, or an ox bellow when it has lots to eat? Of course not, they are heard only when they are suffering from hunger.

Can that which is unsavory be eaten without salt? Is there any taste in the slime of the purslane? The things that my soul refused to touch are now my sorrowful meat.

[Salt is a metaphor for happiness, and "that which is unsavory", or the "slime of the purslane" are metaphors for Job's life. Purslane is a potherb, and the slime of a purslane is an insipid and repulsive food.[1] "My sorrowful meat" is a metaphor for his preoccupation with the thought of death. In effect, Job is asking: can an unsavory life like mine be lived without any happiness? And, if there is no happiness in my life, but only suffering, then why should I struggle to live it? What I would never have considered in the past, I now think about constantly, namely – the desirability of death.[2] It has become my sorrowful meat. Job then continues.]

I do wish that God would give me death, because then, at least, I would have this consolation: that I have always obeyed the words of the Holy One. It is my only joy in my unrelenting pain. As it is, why should I hope? What prospects are there for me? I have nothing, and I am too weak to even help myself.

A despairing man should have the devotion of his friends, even if he were to forsake the fear of the Almighty. But you are as unreliable as streams in the desert. Caravans are confident that they exist, but when they arrive to drink, they are distressed, and disillusioned because the streams are dry. I had hoped for your love and support, but I have been profoundly disappointed.

You saw my dreadful suffering, but you were afraid to tell the truth, i.e., God is punishing a righteous man. I have never asked anything of you, but I am asking you now to be honest. I know that honest words can be painful, but your criticisms are not truthful. Do you mean to correct me, and discard the words of a despairing man? You have traded away my integrity, because you think that in blaming me you have gained God's approval.

Look at me. Would I lie to your face? Do not be unjust. Stop assuming my guilt, and reconsider what you said, because my good name is at stake. Am I not in the best position to know whether my conduct has been blameless? Have you seen any wickedness in my words?

I am not struggling because I am evil. All human life is a struggle: like that of a tired slave looking for evening shade, or a deserving hired man waiting eagerly for his wages.

I have been suffering like this for months. I cannot sleep. My body is clothed with worms and scabs, and my skin is broken and festering. I am disgusting. I have no hope.

O God, remember that my life is short, and I will never see happiness again. Your eye that now sees me, will see me no longer; you will look for me, but I will be no more.

[Job is particularly upset by the suggestion that God was punishing him because he was born with a sinful nature. Throughout his adult life he had obeyed God's commands, and he had expected to be blessed accordingly. If God intended to punish him anyway for something that he could do nothing about, then why would God require his obedience? And what would be the point in seeking God's approval? If he was being punished with suffering, because he was born an evildoer, then there was no way out. He was trapped. Therefore, in an increasingly sarcastic manner, he continues his diatribe against God.]

I will speak from anguish and bitterness. Am I a devil that I must be guarded?[3] When I lie down, I hope my bed might comfort me, but then you frighten and terrify me with dreams and visions of what you might do. I would prefer strangling and death, rather than this body of mine. I despise my life. I do not want to suffer like this. Leave me alone.

What is man that you should value him so highly, and that you should set your heart on him? Is it so that you can search for his sins every morning, and test him every moment? Why don't you leave me alone for even an instant? How have I wronged you, O preserver of men? Why have you set me up so that I have become a burden to myself? If I have sinned, why don't you simply pardon my transgressions and take away my iniquity, because soon I will be dead, and you will search for me, but I will be no more. (Chapters 6,7)

[Despite his initial response, Job quickly recovered, and began to challenge my underlying beliefs and conclusions.
1. Belief: All people are born with a sinful nature, i.e., wicked, and are therefore evildoers.
   Challenge: I am not an evildoer. In fact, if I were to die, then at least I would have this consolation: "that I have obeyed the Holy One."
2. Belief: The wicked suffer hardship.
   Challenge: People such as slaves and hired men also suffer hardship, but not because they were born wicked.
3. Belief: You are being punished because you have actually sinned.
   Challenge:
   a) You say that I have sinned, because you are afraid to admit that God is punishing a righteous man.
   b) What evidence do you have of any sin that I committed? Stop assuming that I have sinned.

c) Why would I lie to you? I am dying. What would I gain from a lie? Besides, am I not in the best position to know whether my conduct has been blameless?

d) People are highly valued by God, and He has set His heart on them. Surely that is not for the purpose of searching for sin.

I had argued that Job was being punished because he was born with a sinful nature, and therefore, just as sparks fly up from a fire, it was a certainty that he had sinned. Job disputes this claim, and the best translation of his challenge is from the King James Version. In addressing God, Job asks: "Why hast thou set me as a mark against thee, so that I am a burden to myself?"[4] In other words, why would you set me up for punishment, by making me bear a burden of sin and wickedness arising out of my human nature? Do you intend to punish me (set me up as a mark) for something I was born with? Is that the purpose of my existence?

But Job also had a problem. In his response he had expressed his belief that his suffering came from the hand of God. If his suffering came from the hand of God, and if it was not punishment for his sin, then why was he suffering?]

[**Bildad** was the next to speak. He and I were not only friends, we were also related – Abraham was our great-grandfather. My ancestry however, went through Sarah, Abraham's wife, while he was a descendent of Keturah, Abraham's concubine.[5] Consequently, there were times when I thought I had a more legitimate connection to Abraham – until he pointed out, that I also had a concubine.[6]

He was a historian, a traditionalist, and a person who firmly believed that God always punishes un-confessed sins. The greater the sin, the greater the punishment, and judging from Job's calamitous circumstances, his sins must have been egregious. We knew each other well. I could see from his body language that he was surprised that Job had maintained the fiction that he was a righteous man. I wondered what he would say.]

You speak nonsense. How long will you insist that you are righteous? Your words are a blustering wind. God does not pervert justice. He does not punish people for nothing. When your children died, they must have sinned, so their punishment was well deserved. If you plead with the Almighty, and if you are blameless in conduct and upright in character, He will respond to you, and make your home prosperous.

Look to the former generations, and learn from their accumulated wisdom. We know so little compared to them. They will teach you that people cannot prosper on their own. Those who ignore God are like the papyrus plant. Without water they wither more quickly than grass. Their confidence hangs by a thread because they believe in themselves. They cling to their possessions for security, but it won't last. Their hopes will shrivel away. Like a green plant, growing among the rocks in the heat of the sun, they will be forgotten and replaced.

You feel rejected, but God does not reject a man whose conduct is blameless. Neither does He strengthen the hands of those whose nature is evil. Nonetheless, if you plead with God, you will find laughter, joy and respect. (Chapter 8)

[I was relieved that Bildad obviously felt the same way I did. Job was attributing his suffering to God when in fact he should have ascribed it to his own sin. If he had not sinned God would not punish him. His argument was as follows:

1. God punishes the wicked because He is just.
2. God not only punishes the wicked with death (as was the case with the children) but also with poverty (as in Job's case.)
3. God not only restores the innocent to prosperity, but He also causes them to be happy.

Because Bildad believed that it was inevitable that everyone would sin by virtue of their sinful nature, he felt justified in saying: "your children <u>must</u> have sinned so their punishment was well deserved." This statement was especially hurtful, and although I agreed with it, I wish that he had mellowed it in some way. In my speech I had referred to the children as well, but I had not accused them of any personal sins.

Bildad had no evidence of any particular sins that the children might have committed. He was relying entirely on his theology when he said it. I knew Job's children, (the seven sons better then the daughters) but from what I could tell, they were all commendable people. I also had seven sons.[7] All were worthy of my admiration. I cannot begin to comprehend the pain of losing any of them, let alone losing them all at the same time. I now cringe to think of the burden of hurt we threw upon a person already overburdened by suffering.

What we did not know at that time, was that Job had tried hard to atone for any sins that his children may have committed. His efforts are described as follows: On their birthdays, Job's sons would invite their three sisters to eat and drink with them. "When the period of feasting had run its course, Job would send for them. Early in the morning he would sacrifice a burnt offering for each of them, thinking 'perhaps my children sinned and cursed God in their hearts.' This was Job's regular custom." (Chap. 1:4,5) Bildad's statement likely caused him to wonder whether he had not done enough to spare his children.]

[**Job** ignores the reference to his children, at least for now, and begins his response by agreeing in part. However, he steadfastly rejects the notion that he was born an evildoer.]

I know that you are right in principle when you say that God will not reject a blameless man. But how can a mortal man be declared blameless before God?

God's wisdom is profound and His power is vast. He causes mountains to erupt, and the earth to quake. He speaks and the sun is eclipsed, or the clouds cover the sky. He spread out the heavens and made the constellations. He does great things too marvelous to understand, and yet when He passes me, I cannot see Him; when He goes by, I cannot perceive Him. When He snatches someone in death: who can stop him? Who dares to say: "what are you doing?" He is almighty, and He does what He wants.

So who am I that I should argue with Him? Though I am innocent, I could only plead for mercy. And why would He change His mind? He has already attacked me, and wounded me without cause. Though I am blameless, He would pronounce me guilty. If it is a question of strength, He wins: if justice, who dares to summon Him? Anyway, it doesn't matter anymore. I despise my life.

You say that God punishes the wicked, but the fact is, God treats both the blameless and the wicked the same – He destroys them both. When a plague strikes, He mocks the despair of the innocent. When a country falls into the hands of the wicked, He blindfolds its judges, so that the innocent also have no justice. If it is not God who does this, then who does?

Oh God, if I was born an evil person, then I am afraid that all my sorrows will continue, because then you cannot hold me innocent. Moreover, if I was born wicked, then why should I try to live a righteous life? The effort would be in vain. Even if I were washed clean and disinfected, you would plunge me into the slime pit. That is to say, even if my actual sins were completely washed away, you would still consider me evil.

[Note. Throughout the Old Testament, and particularly in the Psalms and Proverbs, the "pit" is a metaphor for a place of evil and corruption. For example, in Psalm 55:23, King David declares: "But you, O God, will bring down the wicked into the pit of corruption."

Job is frustrated because he cannot change what he was born with. He is condemned by circumstances for which he was not responsible; over which he has no control, and which he could not change, even if he wanted to. Returning now to Job's speech.]

If only there were an arbitrator. Then I would say to God: do not condemn me, but tell me what charges you have against me. Does it please you to oppress me, to spurn the work of your own hands, while you smile on the schemes of the wicked? What do you have to gain by causing me to suffer? Are your eyes like those of a human ... that you must quickly probe after my guilt and search for my sin? You know that I am not wicked.

[Note, although Job is ostensibly speaking about humans generally, he is actually referring to us. We were after all, the only ones doing the probing and searching. He believed that we had, without any evidence, quickly arrived at the conclusion that he must have sinned, because of his sinful nature. So in a dramatic voice, Job is asking God whether He will also, "quickly probe for my guilt," and condemn him, as we had? If God does, then Job acknowledges, "although you know that I am not guilty, no one can rescue me from your hands."[8]]

Job continues: It was your hands that made me, and fully fashioned me. Will you now turn and destroy me? Remember that you molded me like clay. Will you now turn me to dust again? You guided my conception, and formed me in the womb. You clothed me with skin and flesh, and knit my bones and sinews together. You gave me life and showed me kindness, and in your providence watched over my spirit.

I knew that you were watching me, and if I sinned, you would not let my offence go unpunished. But, even though I am innocent, I cannot lift my head because I am full of shame. If I hold my head up, you may display your powers against me. Again and again you bring new sufferings. If my tribulations are punishment for my evil nature, then why did you cause me to be born?

I wish I had been stillborn, or that I had never been conceived. Hopefully my days are almost over, but until then, turn away from me so I can have a moment's joy. (Chapters 9,10)

[After his initial conciliatory remarks, Job again challenges our beliefs.

1. Belief: God punishes the wicked with suffering and poverty, and causes the innocent to prosper.
Challenge: Job points to the reality in society to demonstrate that God treats both the wicked and the innocent the same. When a plague strikes, it destroys both the wicked as well as the innocent.
2. Belief. God punishes the wicked with suffering
Challenge. When the wicked rule the innocent suffer. Therefore, how can it be said that my suffering is the punishment for my sins, if the innocent also suffer?
3. Belief: God punishes those whose nature is evil.
Challenge:
   a. If the consequence of my birth is, that I should be punished with suffering and ultimately with death, then why did God give me life in the first place?
   b. If I was born wicked, then what is the point of trying to live a righteous life?
   c. God made me, so would He now spurn the work of His own hands?
   d. God gave me life and showed me kindness, so why would He now want to destroy me?

Job defends his contention that he is righteous by disclosing his motivation. He argues: I am righteous, because I knew that God was watching me, and if I sinned He would punish me.]

[**Zophar**, the youngest of us, joins what was now a full-blown dispute. I knew him to be somewhat impulsive and always outspoken. I was sure that he would agree with us, and I was hopeful that he would be respectful of an older man, as was required in our culture. My hope soon vanished]

Are we going to allow your multitude of words to go unanswered? Do you think your lies will be accepted? When you mock God, shall no man make you ashamed? Your words must be answered. Someone must rebuke you when you say that despite your innocence, God has caused you to suffer. You say, your beliefs are flawless, and you are clean in God's sight. Do you understand the extent of the wisdom and the power of God? How I wish that God, who is infinitely wise and powerful, would speak, and disclose to you what He knows. If He did, you would learn that what He knows has two sides:

1. Your actual sins are so many; He has probably forgotten some of them.
2. If God chooses to bring judgment against you because of your sinful nature, who can hinder Him? Surely He recognizes corrupt men, and when He sees their actual sins, does He not take note?

(The KJV translates this passage as follows: "for He knoweth vain men: He seeth (their) wickedness also."[9] Vanity is an attribute of a person's nature, whereas "wickedness that can be seen," describes conduct.)

Vain men like you, think they are wise, but actually they are as stubborn as a wild ass's newborn colt. If you really want to be wise, then prepare your heart, stretch out your hands, and acknowledge the wickedness that dwells within you. Then you will be able to lift your head without shame or fear. Your suffering will be only a memory. Your future will be bright. You will be secure and hopeful, and you will have your rest. You will be respected.

But the wicked will not escape punishment. There is no hope for them. (Chapter 11)

[I was disappointed that Zophar had ignored our cultural requirements, but as to what he said, I thought he was right. He appeals to the nature of God in an attempt to defeat Job's assertion that he is not an evildoer. His argument is:

1. Because God is omniscient, he recognizes everything, including your deceitful nature, and he takes note. Wicked and deceitful people inevitably sin, and you have probably sinned so often that God has forgotten most of them.
2. God is also almighty, and when He chooses to punish the wicked, who can stop Him?
3. You were born like a wild ass's colt, i.e. stubborn by nature. But if you now acknowledge your sinful nature and confess your actual sins, God will restore you.]

[**Job** is visibly angry by what he heard. He now realizes that this is not a casual conversation, so he begins to counter attack in earnest, and to aggressively defend himself. He was obviously and understandably offended by the younger man's impudence, and he responds sarcastically.]

No doubt you are the people with all the wisdom, and wisdom will surely die with you. I have understanding as well as you, and I am not inferior to you. Who doesn't know all these things?

You laugh at me, because I call on God and expect an answer. You laugh even though I am righteous and blameless. Men like you, with nothing to do and no concerns, have contempt for the unfortunate, and for those who are slipping into despair.

You say that God punishes evil people with suffering. But there are people who disobey God, and others who provoke Him, and some who worship other Gods. Yet God has not touched them, as He has me. How can you say that I am being punished with suffering because I am an evil person, when really evil people do not suffer?

You all say that my suffering is a result of my sins, but ask the animals, or the birds, or the fish. They have not sinned, yet they also suffer. And when they suffer they all know that the hand of the Lord has done this. In His hand is the life of every creature, and the breath of all mankind.

Does not the ear distinguish words, and does not the mouth differentiate tastes? It is true that wisdom is found among the aged, and understanding is acquired with age, but true wisdom, strength, counsel and understanding belong to God.

[I pause here to note three points that Job wants to make.
1. He, along with the rest of us, was convinced that his suffering came from the hand of God. The only issue was: why? We believed that his suffering was punishment, both for his evil nature, and for his actual sins. But Job vigorously disagrees. He argues that he is no different than the birds and animals. Their suffering also comes from the hand of God, but they were not evil, and had not sinned. So how could we say that suffering was punishment for sin?
2. The ability to hear and taste are senses shared by almost all people. And just as the ear and the mouth have the capacity to discriminate sounds and tastes, so too, people have some understanding – and hence some capacity to discern truth from fiction. In other words, Job is asking that, in respect to his righteousness, we apply our common sense.
3. Job then addresses an issue that Bildad had raised before. He states: You urged me to look to the former generations for understanding. Well let me tell you. It is true that wisdom and understanding are acquired with age, but to God belongs true wisdom and power: counsel and understanding. Obviously Job was playing a game of one-up-man-ship. Bildad would have been the first to admit that understanding belongs to God. His point was that God uses wise people from previous generations to

convey His counsel. Job then redirects his attention to Zophar.]

You say that God is almighty and in complete control of everything. Of course He is. What you know, I also know. I am not inferior to you. Everything that happens, to all mankind is caused by Him. All nations and their leaders are under His control. I have seen all this and I understand it.

But I still want to talk to the Almighty and argue my case. You however, have smeared me with lies. All of you are worthless healers. If only you would be altogether silent. For you, that would be wisdom.

You say that I am the cause of my own suffering. You are afraid that if you blamed God, He would be angry with you, and He would then punish you as well. But you cannot deceive God as you might a man. He will surely rebuke you if you secretly say things, simply because you are afraid of Him, and of what He might do to you. All of your maxims and proverbs are self-serving.

As for me, I want to be honest with God – come what may. Even if He kills me, my hope is in Him. I am an upright and blameless man, and I want to defend my ways to His face. In fact, that may turn out to be my deliverance, because a hypocrite would not dare come before Him. I know I will be vindicated. If anyone can find anything against me, then I will keep silent and die.

But first O God, grant me two things, and then I will not hide from you.
1. Take away this suffering, and
2. Take away the fear of what you might do.

Then call me, and I will speak; or let me speak, and you will answer. If I am wicked by nature, then show me my wickedness, and the sins that I have committed. Why, O God, do you consider me to be your enemy? Will you break a windblown leaf like me, and chase after my insignificant wrongs? If my friends are correct, and I was born with a sinful nature – certain to sin; then you have written bitter things against me, and make me inherit the sins of my youth.

Do you keep watch on all my paths, and put marks on the soles of my feet, so that you can monitor where I have been, and what sins I have committed? If you do, then people waste away like something rotten, like a garment eaten by moths.

[Job then directly addresses the issue of a sinful nature.] "Man born of a woman is of few days and full of trouble. He springs like a flower and withers away: like a fleeting shadow, he does not endure. Do you fix your eyes on such a one? Will you bring him before you for judgment? Who can bring what is pure from the impure? No one! Man's days are determined: you have decreed the number of his months, and have set limits he cannot exceed."[10]

[Note that Job does not deny that people have a sinful nature: rather he affirms it. His argument is that aging, death, and a life full of trouble, are already the penalty for a sinful nature. Does God want to bring people to judgment, and punish them again for what they were born with? He has already restricted their days, and set limits on what they can do. So leave them alone. Don't punish them again for what they are. He then continues.]

At least there is hope for a tree. It also suffers when it is cut down, but it will sprout again. Its roots remain alive and at the scent of water, it will grow again. But when man dies, that's it. Unlike the tree, he will not grow again.

Oh God, if only you would treat me like you do the tree. Lay me dormant in the grave for a while, and conceal me until the time allotted to my suffering is passed. Then at least I would have hope, because during the course of my suffering, I would know that one day I would be renewed. And then you will call me, and I will answer you. You will desire me, the creature your hands have made. Then you will not count my steps, or mark the soles of my feet to see where I have been, just to keep track of my sins. My offenses will be sealed in a bag, and my sinful nature will be sewn shut.

Instead, just as a mountain erodes and crumbles, and a rock is removed from its place; just as water wears away stones, and torrents wash away the topsoil; you wear people down, and you destroy their hope. You overpower man with misfortune, and you leave him in misery. When his sons are honored or dishonored he doesn't know it, because he feels only the pain of his own body, and mourns only for himself.

Job ends his response by praying that God's punishment will pass and that he will be restored. He then makes an absolutely remarkable claim. "You will call, and I will answer you; you will long for the creature your hands have made."[11] (Chapters 12 – 14)

[Job was obviously getting increasingly frustrated. Perhaps he was getting tired of the personal attacks on himself and his children, and he is fighting back with purpose.

He continues to challenge our underlying beliefs. However, unlike us, he does not rely on his religious beliefs. Instead he relies on reality.

1. Belief: God punishes the wicked with suffering.
   Challenge:
   a. Look at the wicked (included those who serve other gods): they sin but don't suffer.
   b. Look at the birds, the animals, and the fish: they suffer but don't sin. So how can you say that my suffering is the punishment for sin?
2. Belief: God is almighty, and everything that happens is under His control.
   Challenge: If everything is under the control of God, then how can it not be true that suffering comes from the hand of God?
3. Belief: You have sinned, and therefore you are the cause of your own suffering.

Challenge: You say that, because you are afraid that God will be angry with you if you told the truth, i.e., God is punishing an innocent man.

Although Job is convinced that his suffering is not the result of his sin, he does believe that God is causing him to suffer, and he wants to know why. Specifically he wants to inquire of God:

1. Regarding his actual sins: If I am being punished because of my actual sins, then show me what I have done wrong.
2. Regarding his sinful nature:
   a. You have already imposed limits on human beings, such as aging and death. Do you want to punish them again for what they were born with?
   b. You made me. Am I now being punished for what I am?
   c. If I am being punished because of what I am, then why was I born in the first place?
3. Regarding the certainty to sin. As noted, Job concedes that he has a sinful nature. What he disputes is that his sinful nature creates a certainty to sin, which is what we believed. He argues that he is a righteous man, but if we are correct, then "God writes down bitter things against me, and makes me inherit the sins of my youth."[12] The phrase "write down bitter things against me," is an idiomatic way of saying that the sentence has been written. In other words, if we were right, and his sinful nature created a certainty to sin, then the sin that he is being sentenced for, must be the sins of his youth.
4. Regarding the nature of God. What kind of a God are you? Are you a faultfinder, or a God that longs for the creatures that your hands have made?

Finally, on two occasions Job declared: "I am not inferior to you."[13] The question is: why did Job say so?

We had argued that suffering was evidence of sinfulness, and prosperity evidence of righteousness. Job was no longer prosperous, and hence there was no evidence of his righteousness. But Bildad, Zophar and I were prosperous, which by implication meant that we were more righteous than he.

Job counters by affirming that he is not inferior to us. But he did not say so for the purpose of elevating his status, or defending his intelligence, which were never in question. Instead it was said for the purpose of disputing the validity of our argument. He concludes by portraying our arguments as: "platitudes as valuable as ashes, and our defenses as fragile as a clay pot."[14]]

CHAPTER 3

THE GREAT DEBATE: ROUND 2

Eliphaz [Job's denials were causing me to become increasing annoyed. We had known him to be wise, albeit somewhat arrogant man, but now he was showing himself to be a stubborn, self-obsessed narcissist, unwilling to do the right thing. It wasn't as if God was asking a lot from him. If he wanted to be restored to his former self, all he had to do was acknowledge whatever wrong he had done. All three of us had emphasized God's willingness to forgive, but if Job would not confess his sins, then perhaps it was time to emphasize God's punishments.]

Would a wise man utter worthless knowledge? Would he reason with unhelpful talk, and give speeches that can do no good? You even undermine piety and hinder devotion to God by what you say. Your evil nature prompts your crafty speech. Your own words testify against you, and condemn you. Who do you think you are? Do you listen in on God's council, and do you have a monopoly on wisdom?

[I then decided to defend Bildad. He had attempted to convince Job by appealing to the wisdom of our ancestors. In our society former generations are highly respected, but Job had sarcastically responded by stating that wisdom and understanding belonged to God. That was of course true, but I was not about to let Job, summarily dismiss my friend.]

What do you know that we don't know? The gray-haired and the aged are on our side, men even older than your respected father.

God has promised that if you confess your sins, He will restore you. Is that not enough for you? What secret sin are you hiding, that you should turn your spirit against God, and permit such words out of your mouth?

What is mankind, that he could be pure, or one born of woman, that he could be righteous? If God places no trust in his holy ones, if even the heavens are not pure in His eyes, how much less man, who is detestable and corrupt, who drinks up evil like water.[1]

Listen to me, and I will tell you what I have seen, and what I have learned from wise men. [Once again I described what I had seen and learned, as if I were speaking generally of the wicked. However, I was really describing Job's calamitous circumstances, and what I thought his punishment would be. I will now dispense with the charade.]

You will experience the suffering that the Almighty has stored up for you. You do not know the day of your death, but every remaining day you will suffer torment. Terrifying sounds fill your ears. When all seemed well, marauders attacked you. You know you cannot escape His punishment, and that you are marked for death. You wander about in a body fit for vultures. Distress and anguish fill you. You are terrified, like a king poised to attack. You shake your fist at God, and vaunt yourself against the Almighty. When you were fat, you defiantly set yourself against God by relying on your status, and your prosperity. But now you live in a hovel that no one would want to live in. It is ready to become a heap. Hopefully you will not deceive yourself by trusting your capabilities. It is worthless. If you do, you will get nothing in return. Your punishment must be paid in full. When your children were destroyed you became like a vine stripped of its unripe grapes. Your life is fruitless, and without hope and purpose.[2]

God lays desolate those who are hypocrites, and fire consumes the homes of those who love bribes.

The wicked conceive sin, their womb fashions deceit, and they give birth to evildoers. (Chapter 15)

[Job had asserted that he was righteous, and God was punishing an innocent man. But to accuse God of punishing an innocent man is itself a sin.

However, my main argument was that Job could not be righteous. He was "born of a woman" which meant that he was born vile and corrupt; who drinks up evil like water. It is in the nature of all people to be so. Already in the womb they conceive sin, and fashion deceit. They give birth to evildoers who assuredly sin.

Further, God will not restore those who do not confess their sin. Rather they will experience the punishment that God has "stored up for them."]

[**Job** responds in kind. He was profoundly disappointed in us, and in his upcoming speech he refers to us as: "these men." He had expected sympathy and encouragement, but instead he was told that his inexpressible pain and suffering would continue. He vacillates between describing his dire circumstances, and expressing his dismay at our lack of understanding.]

You miserable comforters, will your long-winded speeches never end? If you were in my place, I could speak against you, and shake my head at you, but I wouldn't. Rather, I would encourage you, and try to comfort you, and bring you relief.

O God, you have worn me out; you have devastated my entire household. As if to prove I have sinned, you've reduced me to wrinkled skin and protruding bones. My body is testimony of your displeasure. Men jeer at me and strike me with scorn.

[In our culture, to be fat was a status symbol representing prosperity and success. It was an affirmation of God's favor. But Job was gaunt, and extremely emaciated. Every bone in his body appeared to be exposed. Even he believed that his skeletal appearance was an expression of God's disapproval.]

Continuing: at one time all was well with me, but God made me His target, and crushed me. Without pity, He afflicted my body. Again and again He came at me, and now I am completely destroyed.

I have covered my body in sackcloth, and my strength lies in the dust. My face is red from weeping. But in spite of all my suffering, I have done no wrong, and my prayer is pure. Even now, I know that the witness to my truthfulness is in heaven, and He knows my record.

These men scorn me, even as my eyes pour out tears to God. I will soon die, and I need someone to mediate between God and me, as one would mediate between friends. But these men mock me. I see their hostility.

Oh God, promise to hear me. Pay whatever security is necessary to assure a fair hearing. These mockers have no understanding, and surely you will not allow them to triumph. A man who does not speak the truth, even the eyes of his children will fail.

They denounce me because they think that if they speak on behalf of God, He will reward them. But it is God himself who has made me an object of scorn, such that people spit in my face. My eyes are dim by reason of sorrow, and I am only a shadow of my former self. Truly upright people are appalled at what happened to me, and the innocent are horrified by the hypocrisy of these men.

My days have passed, my plans are shattered, and so are the desires of my heart. Even though these men know I am righteous, they say I am corrupt. They claim that if I simply confess my sins, my health and prosperity can be restored. They have turned night into day. In the face of darkness they say light is near.

They say I was born wicked and corrupt. But if I say to corruption, "you are my father, and to the worm you are my mother or my sister, where then is my hope?"[3] If I am as described by these men, then my hope will descend with me into the grave, and together we will turn into dust. (Chapters 16,17)

[When one gets past Job's personal attacks against us, and the description of his terrible circumstance, the essence of his argument is as follows. He again denies that his suffering is the result of his sin. Instead, he contends that it is the result of God's anger against him, although he does not understand why.

In respect to his assertion that he is innocent, he states:

1. God is my witness, and if God spoke we would know that he was innocent. This was obviously said to contradict Zophar's claim that if God spoke, He would disclose that Job was not only sinful by nature, but also that his actual sins were so many, that He had already forgotten some of them.
2. If all people have a sinful nature by virtue of their birth, and God punishes all who are wicked, then what is there to hope for?

Also, Job's statements: "the eyes of his children will fail," and "they have turned night into day,"[4] require some context.

<u>Regarding: The eyes of the children will fail.</u> I do not believe that Job was wishing our children harm because we had betrayed him, by accusing him of sin. Rather, he is suggesting that children have no hope, if their parents are untruthful. The phrase: "the eyes will fail," is an idiomatic way of saying there is no hope. Zophar used this idiom when he said: "the eyes of the wicked will fail … and their hope shall die."[5] Similarly, in his final address Job states: "if I have caused the eyes of the widow to fail," (i.e., if I have deprived the widow of hope) then I should be punished.[6]

<u>Regarding: They have turned night into day.</u> Prior to this statement, Job relates how he, an innocent man, had prayed to be restored. He discloses that he had clothed himself in sackcloth, and his face was foul from weeping. He believes that notwithstanding his pleas, he will never be restored. He concedes: "my days have passed, my plans are shattered, and so are the desires of my heart."[7] In other words, he, a righteous man, has no hope.

In the meantime, we had accused him of being evil and corrupt, but that despite his corruption, his health and prosperity could be restored if he confessed his sins. Consequently, as a corrupt man, he had hope, but as a righteous man, he was hopeless. From Job's point of view, we had turned night into day.]

[**Bildad** is completely frustrated and his response becomes even more acrimonious as he predicts what he believes will be Job's destiny. In my experience, disputes are often unpleasant affairs, but because Job was our friend, this dispute had become more distressing than most.]

Be sensible, and then we can talk. Your anger consumes you. Is the earth to be abandoned, or a rock removed for your sake? [This is a sarcastic reference to Job's comment that if people are born wicked, and God punishes the wicked, then just as mountains crumble and a rock is removed from its place, so God destroys hope.[8] In effect, Bildad is asking whether God's moral order is changed for Job's sake. It is not God who destroys hope, but the wicked. He then continues by describing the consequence of Job's wickedness.]

God has snuffed out your lamp because you are wicked, and the flame of your life has stopped burning. Darkness is creeping over you, and your strength is lost. Your own schemes have taken you down. New terrors come at you, and dog your every step. Calamity awaits you, and disease eats away at your skin. Death is devouring your limbs. Your home provides you with no comfort or security. You will meet the king of horrors. Your tent must be disinfected. When you die, no one will remember you. You have no children to survive you, and no one to carry on your name.[9]

So severe will be your suffering that the men from the west will be appalled, and the men from the east will be horrified. Such is the fate of an evil man. (Chapter 18)

[In all our previous speeches, we had assured Job that if he acknowledged his sin, he would be restored. I note with interest that Bildad had concluded that Job would never confess his sins. As a result he doesn't even mention that confession is the pathway to restoration. He simply describes the destiny of the wicked, which he believes Job to be.

His reference to men from the west and east (who were considered enemies) is another sarcastic reference to Job's words. Job had said that the upright would be appalled, and the innocent horrified, by the injustice that he was experiencing. Bildad turns these words around to say that Job's punishment would be so severe, even his enemies would be appalled and horrified.]

[**Job** is not prepared to capitulate, but perhaps to deescalate the rising animosity, he does become somewhat more conciliatory. He probably realizes that the debate had degenerated, and he attempts to bring it back to a higher level. He describes in detail his loss, and begs for our understanding and fellowship. He again addresses us as: "my friends."]

Shamelessly you attack me. If it is true that I have gone astray, my error remains my concern only. If you exalt yourself, and use my humiliation against me, then bear in mind that it was God who wronged me, and sent me this suffering. I cry out at this injustice, but he has walled me in so that I cannot pass.

God has stripped me of power and respect, and destroyed my hope. He is angry with me, and treats me like His enemy. He has surrounded me with calamities. He has alienated my relatives from me, and my acquaintances are estranged. My servants consider me a stranger, and when I call they do not answer. Even when I beg, they will not respond. My breath is offensive to my wife, and my own brothers find me disgusting. Even young children despise and mock me. My associates abhor me, and those I loved have turned against me. My bones stick to my skin, and I am near death. Therefore, have pity on me my friends, for the hand of God has struck me. Why do you persecute me as God has done? Is my physical suffering not enough for you?

Oh that my words be written in a book, or better yet that they be inscribed into a rock forever. The reason for this desire, is that I know that my Redeemer lives, and in the end, He will stand upon the earth, but by that time I may be to weak to speak. Although my body may be destroyed, I know that with my own eyes I will see God. How my heart yearns within me, because then I will know why He has done this to me, and I will be vindicated. I am overwhelmed at the thought.[10]

If you are hounding me because you believe that the root of the problem lies within me, then be afraid. You are also human, and you too will face His judgment. (Chapter 19)

[Job counters our belief, that all those born of a woman are wicked, and God punishes the wicked with suffering. He reaffirms his belief that his suffering is not caused by his sin; but by God's anger, although he does not understand why. Nonetheless, because God knows him to be innocent, he believes that before he dies, he will be vindicated. He warns: if we believe he is wicked because of his nature, then we should be afraid, because we are also human, and as such have a sinful nature. As a result, we too are subject to God's punishment.]

[**Zophar** immediately understands the implication of Job's warning. He is offended that Job had suggested that he might also be exposed to God's punishment. He completely ignores Job's plea for fellowship.)

I hear a rebuke that dishonors me, and I must respond. Surely you know, what everyone has known since ancient times; the joy of the wicked is brief. Though his pride reaches the heavens, he will eventually die. His influence will vanish, and he will be forgotten. His body will disintegrate like his own dung. His wealth will be dispersed, and his children will be required to make amends.

To the wicked, evil is sweet. They hide it under their tongue, and they cannot bear to let it go. But it will become a poison within them. They will eventually lose the benefit of their sins, and happiness will elude them. The wicked have no respite from their cravings, and they cannot save themselves.

In the midst of plenty, distress, and the full force of misery overtook you. When you had filled your belly, God vent His burning anger against you, and rained down His blows upon you. You tried to flee from His iron weapon, i.e., suffering, but His bronze bow, i.e., death, will pierce you; and you are terrified. God's fire will consume you, and devour what is left in your tent. The heavens will expose your guilt. Such is the fate that God allots to the wicked. It is the heritage appointed for them by God.[11] (Chapter 20)

[Job had consistently refused to acknowledge his sinfulness, so Zophar offers an explanation. He accuses Job of refusing to confess because he wants to be wicked. For Job (like all those born of a woman,) evil is sweet, and he craves it, and cannot let it go. Despite his severe suffering, he refuses to humble himself, and acknowledge his wickedness. Consequently, he will not be forgiven, and he will perish with his sins. Suffering and death is the fate that God allots to the wicked, and there is no escape.]

[**Job's** response is to continue to try to elevate the debate, while at the same time maintaining his righteousness.]

Bear with me while I speak, and after I have spoken continue to mock me if you want. Is my complaint directed at man? I have good reason to be impatient. I am weak and trembling, but the wicked increase in power. Their children are established, while mine are dead. The wicked have no fear, while I am terrified. They are happy and prosperous, while I am destitute. They ignore God and want nothing to do with Him; so why is God not angry with them? They ask: "who is the

Almighty that we should obey Him, and what good will it do to pray?" Why are they not being punished?

[Job next raises – almost as an afterthought – the issue of his children's death, and for a moment he is no longer responding to Zophar. Instead, he is addressing me. You will recall that in my first speech, I stated that the children of fools are punished. Job is now addressing my statement and retorts: "It is said, God stores up a man's punishment for his sons." What good is that? Let God repay the fool himself, so he understands His judgment. Let the fool drink of the anger of the Almighty. What does the fool care about the family he leaves behind, when his allotted months come to an end.

Job knew that I was the one who had made the statement, but he begins his retort by saying: "It is said." In an attempt to mitigate the hurt, I had made it sound as if I was speaking of someone else. Job is now doing something similar to what I had done, by making it sound as if someone else had said it. In so doing he is ridiculing my spurious attempt to lessen the hurt, and letting me know that what I said hurt very much. He then again turns his attention to Zophar.]

Some people (both the wicked and the righteous) die well nourished and prosperous; others die, having never enjoyed anything good; and in the grave, both lie side by side, eaten by the same maggots.

I know what you're thinking. You are wondering why I am no longer prosperous. What have I done to deserve this? You believe that I am being punished with suffering and poverty because I am wicked. If I am destitute because I am wicked, then why do the wicked prosper? I know that you will give me a few individual examples of wicked people who have lost their homes. But ask those who have been around, and they will tell you the truth. Many evil people are allowed to escape disaster. No one criticizes them openly, or retaliates against them. When they die, an honor guard watches over their tomb. Many pay their respects, and they rest in peace. (Chapter 21)

[In his response, Job directly challenges our contention that God always punishes the wicked with suffering. Again he relies on the inescapable reality that, in this life, the wicked are not always punished. On the contrary, they often prosper. In fact, God does not treat the wicked any differently than the innocent. If God does not always punish the wicked with suffering, and if the innocent also suffer, then it cannot be true that suffering is always the punishment for wickedness.]

CHAPTER 4

THE GREAT DEBATE: ROUND 3

Eliphaz [Clearly Job did not lack understanding. What he lacked was the will to change: but why? It wasn't as if his current circumstances were all that desirable. The only explanation was that he loved his sin more than his health. I had no interest in maintaining the friendship of a narcissistic, holier-then-thou individual, who waved his self-declared righteousness like a flag. I decided to be more confrontational.]

You continue to insist that you are righteous. But what pleasure, benefit or gain, could your righteous character give the Almighty? What would God gain by your blameless conduct? Is it for your piety that God rebukes you, and brings this suffering onto you? No! It is because your wickedness is great, and the sins of your heart are endless.

[Up to now, I had argued that he must have sinned because he was born of a woman. I decided that it was time to stop arguing by deduction, and state what I believed to be true – he had sinned. It is true that I didn't know what the sins were, but that really didn't matter. Judging from his punishment they were manifestly serious, so I simply accused him of a number of offences. I now know that my accusations probably marked the low point in our debate, and I deeply regret making them. Even to repeat them causes me sorrow.]

Despite what you say, you demanded security from your brothers for no reason. You stripped men of their clothing, leaving them naked. You refused to give water to the weary, and you withheld food from the hungry. You were a "mighty man," and had everything you needed. Yet you sent widows away empty handed, and you broke the strength of the fatherless. And that is why you are now overcome by the fear of additional and unforeseen suffering, and that is why you are drowning in despair.

You think, because you can't see God, He can't see you: but you are wrong. God is infinite, and knows everything. You cannot hide anything from Him.

Will you continue to walk the path of evil men – with those who have already been discredited, and who say to God: "leave us alone?" If you were righteous, you would be happy to see the wicked destroyed, but you don't want that, because you are also wicked.

Submit to the Almighty and be at peace with Him, and good will come your way. Accept God's law, and lay up His words in your heart. If you return to the Almighty, and remove wickedness from your home, He will build you up. If you acknowledge the sin in your heart, then He will hear you, and your wealth will be restored. (Chapter 22)

[Throughout the debate Job had argued that he was righteous, and therefore could not be the cause of his dreadful circumstances. So I challenged him.
1. Why would God cause you to suffer, if not for your sins? Is it for your piety and blameless ways? What would God gain by your piety? The last question was designed to turn Job's words against him. He had previously asked; what would God gain from my suffering?
2. I accused Job of wanting a relationship with wicked people by again using his words against him. In his previous response to Zophar, Job had described prosperous, albeit wicked people, as those who say to God: "leave us alone."[1] I pointed out that it was actually Job who walked with those who say to God: "leave us alone."]

[**Job** did not react to my unfounded accusations of wrongdoing. He knew he was a righteous man, but he also knew that he could never convince us, especially after what I had said. So he again expresses his desire to speak with God, who alone would know with absolute certainty that he was righteous. He was however, uncertain of God's reaction.]

If only I knew where to find Him, I would present my case. Would God use His power against me? No, I believe He would empower me. I am an upright man, and I would learn why He causes me to suffer. But I cannot find Him. Nonetheless, He knows that my feet have followed His steps, and I have kept to His way. I have obeyed His commands and treasured His words. If I could present my case to Him, I would come out as gold.

On the other hand, once He has made His decision, who can change His mind? He does what He pleases. He will do to me whatever He has planned. He controls my destiny. I am terrified when I think about what else He may have in store for me.

Evil men steal from the poor, making them poorer still. As a result of their evil deeds, the innocent go about naked, hungry and thirsty. They are destitute, and cry to God for help. But God does not punish the evildoer. Why does He not set aside a day of judgment for them? (Chapters 23-24:17)

[**Bildad** tries for the last time to convince Job of his wickedness. However, to his credit, he does not accuse Job of overt sins, as I had so disgracefully done. Rather, he returned to the original theme, i.e., Job was wicked because of his sinful nature. As before, he does not mention the possibility of restoration through confession.]

You say that God does not punish the wicked. Well, the truth is; for a little while they may be exulted, but then they will die and be forgotten. They are like foam on the surface of the water. Everything they own is cursed. However important they seem to be, they will be cut down like ears of corn, and they will not be remembered.

Dominion belongs to God: He is in control of everything. He is powerful and dreadful, and dispenses both blessings and sufferings. He is also omniscient. You seem to think that God cannot see your wickedness. But upon whom does His light not shine?

How can a person be righteous before God? How can one born of a woman be pure? If the stars are not pure in his eyes, how much less is man, who is but a maggot, or a son of man, who is only a worm. (Chapters 24:18 – 25:6[2])

[**Job** had enough, and he tries unsuccessfully to terminate the debate in respect to his wickedness.]

You have enlightened my stupidity. Where did you get all your wisdom?

I know that God is both omniscient and omnipotent. I know God is the Creator, and controls everything on earth and in the heavens. Nothing happens outside of His control.

But He has denied me justice. And I vow by the living God – the one who has caused me to suffer, and embittered my soul – that as long as I live, I will speak no evil, and tell no lies. I will never concede that what you say is correct. I will maintain my righteousness and never let it go. My conscience will be clear as long as I live. (Chapters 26 – 27:6)

[**Zophar** is not deterred by Job's efforts to terminate the debate. In fact he seems eager to prolong it. As can be seen from his last speech, he now sees Job as a sin-loving dissident, who refuses to acknowledge his wickedness. Consequently, he is eager to let Job know what God has in store for him. As was the case with Bildad, Zophar does not raise the possibility of restoration. He too describes the destiny of the wicked, and he clearly as Job in mind.]

You do not want to see the wicked punished, because you too are wicked. As for me, I am happy to see them punished. In fact, may my enemies be punished like the wicked, and my adversaries like those who do evil.

You ask: where is my hope if I am totally corrupt? But I ask: where is the hope of the hypocrite when God takes away his soul?

I will teach you about God's power. Here is the fate God allots to the wicked, and the heritage a ruthless man, like you, receives from the Almighty: the wicked may have many children, but they will all die. They may have money and clothing, but eventually the righteous and upright will divide it up. They may have houses, but they are fragile, and will be blown away in a storm. The wicked man himself will experience the plague. He will be overcome with terror. Eventually he will die, and everyone will mock him. Even his widow will not weep for him. (Chapter 27:7-23[3])

[**Job** answers for the last time and gives a lengthy discourse on wisdom, disappointment, suffering and punishment. He ends by again defending his character and his conduct.] He states:

From some of the most remote and inaccessible places on earth, people find treasures. But where is wisdom found? Where does understanding dwell? Although wisdom and understanding are more valuable than anything on earth, it cannot be found or purchased. It is hidden from every living thing on earth. But God has found it. He tested it and confirmed it to be genuine. And this is what He said to all people: "the fear of the Lord – that is wisdom, and to shun evil – that is understanding." (Chapter28)

How I long for the days when God watched over me; when His lamp shone upon my head, and by His light I walked through darkness; when His intimate friendship blessed my house; when my children were always present; when I was prosperous; when I was respected and honored. I helped the poor and the fatherless, and caused the widow's heart to sing for joy. I dressed myself in righteousness, and justice was my robe. I had anticipated that I would live a long and good life, surrounded by family. (Chapter 29)

Instead I am mocked even by the outcasts; I have no dignity left. I am powerless, vulnerable and frightened. I am depressed and incomprehensively sad. My suffering grips me; the gnawing pain never rests. God has attacked me. My skin is peeling, and my body burns with fever. (Chapter 30)

I have always been truthful, honest and faithful. I have always been mindful that God created everyone, and I treated all people accordingly. I have not sinned. I am righteous. I am prepared to give to God an account of my life. That is my defense and I am prepared to sign my name to it. (Chapter 31)

Summary

If I were to reduce our debate to a power point presentation, and each argument presented in its simplest form, the broad outline would be somewhat as follows. The issue to be resolved was: why was Job suffering so severely?

A. We believed that Job had sinned, and consequently he was being punished with suffering and poverty. (8:4; 15:5,6; 18:5-19; 20:21-25, 29)
B. Job's rebuttal:
What evidence do you have that I sinned? I will be dead soon. What do I gain from lying? (6:24-30).

C. We countered that even if we have no evidence of any actual sin, he was born of a woman, and therefore he was wicked by nature, and subject to God's punishment. (4:7-9,17-20; 5:6,7; 8:3-6; 11:11; 15:14-16; 18:21; 20:29; 22:5; 25:4-6; 27:13)
D. Job's rebuttal
1) Wickedness is not the only cause of suffering. Slaves and hired men also suffer, but not because they are wicked. (7:1,2)

2) "Oh God, What is man that you should magnify him, and that you should set your heart on him?" Surely it is not to examine, and to test him every moment. (7:17,18)

3) God made me, so why would He set me up for punishment, by making me bear a burden of sin and wickedness arising out of my human nature? (7:20)

4) If God punishes with suffering those who are wicked, then why do the innocent also suffer? (9:22-24)

5) If I was born wicked, then what is the point of trying to live a righteous life? (9:29)

6) Oh God, do you find it a good thing to oppress and despise the work of your own hands? Are you like my friends, in that that you search after my wickedness? (10:3-6)

7) God gave me life and showed me kindness, why would He now want to destroy me? (10:8-12)

8) If I was born wicked, and God's real purpose is to punish the wicked, then why was I born in the first place? (10:13-19)

9) If God punishes those who are born wicked, then why are those who provoke God, secure? (12:6)

10) Animals, birds and fish suffer, and they know that their suffering comes from the hand of God. But they are not wicked, so how can it be said that suffering is punishment for man's wicked nature? (12:7-10)

11) You say that God is punishing me with suffering because I am evil. You say that because you cannot bring yourself to say that God is punishing an innocent man. You are speaking wickedly and deceitfully. Do you think you can deceive Him as you might deceive men? Surely He will rebuke you if you secretly show partiality. (13:7-11)

12) If my nature is so wicked that there is a certainty that I have sinned, then, oh God, tell me how many

wrongs and sins I have committed, and show me what they are. (13:23)

13) If people are born wicked, and God punishes the wicked, then they "waste away like something rotten, like a garment eaten by moths." (13:28)

14) So as to restrict man's sinful nature, God has already imposed limits, such as aging and death. Why would He want to punish them again for what they were born with? (14:1-6)

15) God made man, and He longs for the creature that his hands have made. Surely that was not to keep track of their sins, and then to destroy them. (14:15-22)

16) My hands have been free of violence, and my prayer is pure. Even now, the witness to my righteousness and truthfulness is in heaven. (16:17-20)

17) You say that all those born of a woman are corrupt, and in the eyes of God, people are but maggots and worms. But "if I say to corruption, 'You are my father,' and to the worm, 'my mother' or 'my sister,' where then is my hope?" (17:14,15)

18) If I am punished because the root of the problem lies within me, then be afraid because you are also human. (19:28,29)

19) If people are punished because they are wicked by nature, and God always punishes the wicked, then why do evil men, "spend their years in prosperity and go down to the grave in peace, (and why are) evil men spared from the day of calamity?" (21:13,30)

20) You say that I am so inherently wicked, that there is a certainty that I have sinned. But God knows me; He knows the way I have taken, and when He has tested me, I will come out as gold. (23:10-12)

21) If I was born inherently wicked, and God always punishes the wicked, then why did He bless me, watch

over me, and extend His friendship to me, until now? (29:2-4)

22) All those born of a woman are not inherently wicked, vile and corrupt by nature because, "Did not He who made me in the womb, make them? Did not God form us both within our mothers?" (31:15)

E. We argued that God would stop punishing him, and would restore him to health and prosperity, if he confessed his sins. (5:8,27; 8:5-7,21,23; 11:13-19)

F. Job's Rebuttal:
Job overall response was: my character is upright; my conduct is blameless.

G. We then answered by advancing a number of arguments that we believed proved that Job had an evil and corrupt nature, and therefore, could not have been upright and blameless.

1. The "I have observed" argument.
   a. Those who do evil, suffer evil.
   b. You are suffering.
   c. Therefore, you are an evildoer. (4:7-11)

2. The "punishment proves" argument.
   a. God punishes the wicked.
   b. You are being punished.
   c. Therefore, you are wicked. (8:3,4; 11:10-12; 15:5,6)

3. The converse of that argument was also advanced.
   a. God does not punish the innocent.
   b. You are being punished.
   c. Therefore, you are not innocent. (4:7,8; 8:20-22)

4. The "you are mortal" argument
   a. All mortals are wicked.
   b. You are a mortal
   c. Therefore, you are wicked. (5:6,7; 15:16,35; 25:4)

5. The "un-roused God" argument.
   a. God rouses himself if the upright calls.
   b. He did not rouse himself for you.
   c. Therefore, you are not upright. (8:5,6,20)

6. The "ancestors agree" argument
   a. All ancestors agree that a mortal cannot be righteous.
   b. You are a mortal.
   c. Therefore you are not righteous. (8:8-13; 15:7-13)

7. The "lower than the angels" argument
   a. The angels are not blameless.
   b. You are lower than the angels.
   c. Therefore you are not blameless. (4:17-20; 15:14,15)

8. The "your words prove" argument
   a. You say that God punished an innocent man.
   b. That statement is a sin.
   c. Therefore your words prove that you are not righteous. (11:2-6; 15:2-6)

Conclusion

There was no point in going on. In his own eyes, Job considered himself righteous. We were mystified, angry, disappointed, and frustrated. Mystified, that his dire circumstances did not overcome his pride. Angry, because we had always known him to be a good man, and yet he refused to do the right thing. Disappointed, because we were unable to persuade him to acknowledge his sin. Frustrated, that he refused to accept the truth that would have set him free.

We were about to leave when God spoke. He directed His response to Job, but we knew that the message was also intended for us. At first we found His response difficult to understand, but eventually we learned what it was that God was trying to teach us.

Before considering God's response, it may be beneficial to analyze the debate with a view to understanding why God responded as He did. Thereafter, I wish to deal with the alleged appearance of Elihu.

CHAPTER 5

ANALYZING THE DEBATE

Introduction

When we first visited Job, we had no idea that it would end in a dispute. The initial purpose of our visit was to sympathize and comfort our friend. However, Job's question: "why is life given to those who have no future, and whom God has hedged in with suffering?"[1] changed everything. Implicit in the question was the contention that God was responsible for his suffering, and for depriving him of the opportunity to enjoy his life.

We all agreed that Job was suffering terribly, and that God was punishing him. The entire dispute was: why? My friends and I believed that God was punishing him because of his sin, making him the cause of his own suffering.

But he contended that he was a righteous and upright man, and although he also believed that God was punishing him, he did not know why. He insisted that it was not because of his sin, but apart from that he had no idea why God would do so.

When Job said that he was a righteous and upright man, what he meant was: notwithstanding his sinful nature, he had always been obedient and virtuous, both in respect to his conduct, and his nature, and he was determined to defend both. For Job, righteousness described his obedience, and uprightness described his virtuous nature as manifested by his character. He knew that to be upright and righteous, two things were necessary: revere God, and shun evil. His nature was shaped by his reverence for God, and his conduct was governed by his determination to shun evil.

We countered by reminding him that he could neither be righteous nor upright, because he was born of a woman.

Therefore, he was so evil, vile and corrupt, as to create a certainty that he had sinned.

Our View of Human Nature

Although we were familiar with the concept of "human nature," the term was unknown to us. The best we could do was to describe it. Human nature is what we were born with. It is the inherent psychological DNA, common to all people. It is the essence of who we are. It is innate to the human species, and we cannot change it.

When we made reference to all those born of a woman, we were of course, referring to the human species. And when we described all those born of a woman as inherently "evil, vile and corrupt,"[2] we were describing human nature whether we had a term for it or not. It is a general description of all the sins that make up our hereditary nature. These sins include envy, hate, greed, pride, jealousy, etc. These are not sins that describe what a person does: rather, these are sins that describe who a person is.

These are the same sins that are often described as the sins of the heart. They are so described because, in the Bible, the heart is seen as the essence of who a person is. These sins create a completely corrupt nature, shared by all who are born of a woman. Because people do not wish to show themselves as corrupt, these sins are often hidden. I suspected this was true of Job, so in my second speech I asked him; "what secret sin are you hiding?"[3]

In addition to the hidden sins of the heart, there are also overt sins. These are the sins that relate to what a person does, and were described by Zophar as, "sins that can be seen."[4] Overt sins are spawned by the hidden sins of the heart. That is why King Solomon urged his children to, "keep your heart with all diligence; for out of it are the issues of life."[5]

We had no knowledge of any overt sins that Job had actually committed, but there was one thing we believed to be true; i.e., all people are born with an inherently evil nature. Consequently, when God punishes evil, it is not only for what people do, but also for who they are. The only way to escape His punishment is to acknowledge, not only their sinful deeds, but also their sinful nature.

Furthermore, people cannot "will" to be anything different than what they are. It is not that people have no volition. Rather, it is that their volition is enslaved by the sins of the heart. Zophar describes a person's enslavement to sin as follows; "evil is sweet in his mouth, and he cannot bear to let it go. He will have no respite from his craving, and he cannot save himself."[6]

Because peoples' "will" is enslaved by the sins of heart, the only certainty is that they will commit sinful acts. I described it as: just as certain as sparks flying up from a fire.[7]

So when Job insisted that his conduct was blameless, my friends and I realized we would have to convince him otherwise, both for his sake, and the honor of God. Because we had no evidence of any overt sins that Job had actually committed, we had to rely solely on our religious beliefs, i.e., his sinful nature would have caused him to commit sinful acts.

Job's view of Human Nature

During the course of the debate Job did not deny he had a sinful nature. Rather, he affirmed it. But under no circumstances did he believe he was innately and totally evil. He began with the premise that God carefully creates all people, and He does not spurn the work of His hands. On the contrary, God highly values those whom He created, and sets His heart on them. He then makes it personal, and relates that God gave him life, and showed him kindness, and in His providence watched over his spirit.[8]

He believed; because God had created him, it could not be true that already at birth he was enslaved to sin. God is Almighty, always in control, and does what He pleases. If all people were born innately wicked, that would mean that God had made them so, and Job wanted no part of such thinking. He states: *"As long as I have life within me, and the breath of God in my nostrils; my lips will not speak wickedness, and my tongue will utter no deceit. I will never admit that you are right; till I die, I will not deny my integrity. I will maintain my righteousness and never let go of it; my conscience will not reproach me as long as I live."*[9]

Although Job passionately and categorically repudiated our view, he does not expressly articulate what he believed human nature it to be. We had attacked him by saying that he could not be righteous, because he was born evil and corrupt. He had argued (correctly as it turned out) that we were wrong. To achieve his purpose, it was not necessary for him to formulate an alternative view of human nature, and he did not do so.

Nonetheless, it is possible to infer what he believed, from what he did and said. It appears that for Job, human nature created, not a certainty to sin, but rather, a propensity to sin. That was why he offered sacrifices for his children. It was not because he knew them to be evil or evildoers, but because they "may have sinned."[10] The fact that he offered sacrifices "regularly," suggests that he believed human nature created more than the mere possibility to sin.

Neither did he believe that people were destined to remain totally corrupt for the duration of their lives, with no capacity to change. Job pointed to himself as proof that he was not enslaved to sin. Throughout his adult life, he overcame the propensity to sin through the exercise of his will. He believed he was responsible for who he was, and what he did, precisely because he had a choice.[11]

To the extent that Job overcame his sinful nature, he became a person of character and integrity – honest, faithful, loyal, generous etc. His character was a manifestation of his nature.[12]

A Comparative Analysis

Our View	Job's View
1. Human Nature 　a. Is totally evil, vile and corrupt. 　b. It is the essence of who people are. 　c. Hence people are totally evil, vile, and corrupt, from birth till death.	1. Human Nature 　a. Is not totally evil, vile or corrupt. 　b. Wickedness is not the essence of who people are. 　c. People are not totally evil, vile, and corrupt from birth till death.
2. Sins of the Heart. 　a. All the sins of the heart are an intrinsic part of human nature and therefore there is a certainty that people will sin.	2. Sins of the Heart 　a. Although people have a propensity to sin, the sins of the heart can be overcome by an act of the will, and as a result, people can change.
3. The will 　a. The will is enslaved to the sins of the heart.	3. The Will 　a. The will is free to choose good or evil.
4. Overt Sins 　a. Are sins that relate to what people do. 　b. Are spawned by the sins of the heart, and cannot be overcome.	4. Overt sins 　a. These are sins that people choose to do. 　b. They can be overcome by an act of the will.
5. Character 　a. No one can be a person of character, because the sins of the heart cannot be overcome. 　b. They will always be	5. Character 　a. The propensity to sin can be overcome, and hence people can choose to be people of good character.

| evil, vile and corrupt. |

A Sinful Nature and an Upright Character

Before proceeding, I must clarify an issue raised by Job. He acknowledged that all people have a sinful nature, but prior to that he had consistently affirmed his own upright character. How could both be true?

The answer I am about to give would not have been my answer before God accused me of slander. Before God's rebuke, I would have said that both could not be true. However, my chastisement, and my subsequent conversations with Job, completely changed my thinking.

During the debate, we had argued that all people, including Job, are so evil, vile and corrupt, that there was a certainty they would sin. We contended that all people conceive sin, their womb fashions deceit, and they give birth to evildoers who drink up evil like water. They do so because evil is sweet, and they crave it; and are unable to save themselves from their cravings. A person could not "will" not to sin.

If human nature was as evil as we thought it was, Job could not be anywhere near a man of upright character or blameless conduct. Both could not be true. If all those born of a woman are destined to be evildoers, then one person cannot choose to be righteous. If all people cannot be anything other than corrupt, then one person cannot choose to be virtuous. If all people are enslaved to sin, then one person is not free to be upright. That was why I had shifted the focus away from Job and towards human nature. I was sure that as between my view, that human nature is so evil as to create a certainty to sin, and Job's assertion that he was upright, my view would prevail.

I was reassured when my friends agreed. Bildad was of the view that human nature is so evil that Job's children must have sinned, and therefore their punishment was well deserved. Similarly, Zophar believed that because of Job's sinful nature, it was impossible for Job not to have sinned. Consequently, he accused Job of committing so many sins that God had probably forgotten most of them.[13]

In terms of the extent of the corruption, we made no distinction between a person's nature and his character. It wasn't necessary, because a completely evil, vile, and corrupt nature, cannot give rise to a good character.

Job correctly perceived that if we were right, then he was trapped. If evil was an inherent and intrinsic part of his nature, and if he had no capacity to "will" himself to be different, then what was the point of trying to live an obedient life? God controlled everything, and if it were true that he could not be obedient, then why would God require it? Was he born so that God could quickly probe his guilt, and then condemn him?

My friends and I have come to realize and acknowledge our error. We painted all people with the same corrupt brush. In doing so, we made no allowances for the indisputable reality that there are differences in people. We now know, what should have been obvious to us even then, i.e., all people are not morally equivalent. There is no doubt that some people are evil and corrupt. There are others who are upright. Most people fall somewhere in between, but all, including the upright, have the propensity to sin.

This propensity endures for their entire life, but because of a free will, so does their capacity to overcome it. Anyone can choose to become a person of good character, or choose to submit to the sins of their heart. Good people can choose badly, and bad people can choose well. King David is an example of a person of character, yet he chose to commit adultery. On the other hand, the thief on the cross, who throughout his life had submitted to the sins of his heart, chose in the last few moments of his life, to publicly acknowledge Jesus.

Job had, throughout his adult life, "shunned evil." Through his "will", he had overcome the propensity to sin, and became a man of upright character and blameless conduct. It is impossible to become a person of character without a free will.

I now believe the converse of what I once believed. If one person is good, then it cannot be true that all people are evil. If one person is virtuous, then all people cannot be corrupt. If one person is free to be upright, then all people cannot be enslaved to sin.

Although the Bible does not define human nature, it does affirm (through the mouth of God no less) that Job was blameless in conduct and upright in character. Consequently, if Job could not be both upright and completely corrupt, then I admit; the concept that all people are completely corrupt, and remain so for their entire lives, must be wrong.

When Job took issue with our allegation that all people have a wicked nature, it was for the purpose of defending himself. However, he did not do so by making some generalized statements about his good nature. Just as he had asked us to specifically identify his sins, so too, he specifically defends the good attributes of his character. If what we said were true, and everyone was inherently wicked, and remained so for the duration of his or her life, then no one could be a person of good character. Consequently, when Job identifies the specific attributes of his character for which he was respected, he at the same time, refutes our allegation that all people are born with an inherently wicked nature.

In **chapter 29**, Job describes in detail his life prior to his debilitating disease. He relates that he was respected because he was generous, righteous and just (all attributes related to his upright character.) In respect to his conduct, he states that he rescued the poor and the fatherless; and assisted the blind, the lame and the needy. He concludes by again describing the respect, adoration and praise that he received because of who he was, and what he did.

In **chapter 31**, Job once again makes the case he would make, if only God would listen. With his final words he vigorously defends both the purity of his heart, i.e., his nature (as manifest in his character), and his blameless conduct. He discloses that his motivation to have a good heart, and do the right thing was because he respected the splendor of God, and dreaded His destruction. In other words, his reverence for God was the basis of the choices he made.

He states: *If I had lied (conduct), or had a deceitful heart (character), then let God judge me. If I have strayed from His pathway (conduct), or if my heart was jealous (character) for what my eyes have seen, then let others eat the crops that I have planted. If my heart was enticed (character) by a woman; that would be a heinous crime: yes, it would be an iniquity to be punished. If I had been unfair to my servants (conduct), or if my heart had been biased (character), then let God punish me.*

Have I refused to help the poor (conduct), or been selfish (character) with my food? No, since childhood I have cared for the widows, the homeless and the needy (conduct). Have I put my trust in money (character), or gloated about my wealth (conduct)? If I were prideful (character) this also would be an iniquity to be punished. Has my heart been secretly enticed (character) to worship (conduct) anyone other then the God of heaven? Was I happy with the misfortunes of my enemies (character), or have I ever cursed anyone (conduct)?

Job concludes his defense by again directing his attention to human nature generally. He rejects the allegation that his nature is totally vile, evil and corrupt, simply because he was born of a woman. He recognizes that aging, death, a life full of trouble, and other unspecified limitations are already the penalty for a sinful nature, and he resents being punished again for what Adam did. Does God want to bring people to judgment, and punish them again for what they were born with?

He denies having *covered my transgression as Adam did, by hiding mine iniquity in my bosom.* Adams transgression was: in an act of disobedience, he had eaten from the tree of the knowledge of good and evil, an overt sin. However, the iniquity that he hid in his heart, and which gave rise to his act of disobedience, was envy and pride.

Iniquities

I know I may be repeating myself, but because of what follows, it is especially important to remember that we had no evidence of any sins that Job had committed. Consequently, we had to rely on what we believed was true about all people. Human nature is so evil, as to create a certainty that all people (including Job) would sin.

As previous pointed out, the words, "evil, vile and corrupt" are general descriptions of the sum total of the specific sins that make up human nature. Job was an exceptionally skilled debater, and he realized it would be difficult for us to specifically identify any sins, whether hidden or overt, that caused us to accuse him of being evil. As a result, he consistently, and repeatedly demanded that we name the specific sin of which he was accused. Our failure to do so would undermine our most basic assertion, i.e., he was totally corrupt.

During the debate, three root-words were used to represent the hidden sins that, my friends and I believed, are characteristic of human nature. The transliteration of these Hebrew words are: "aven", "avel", and "avon." The King James Version (KJV) properly translates these words as "iniquities" so as to differentiate them from overt sins. The International Standard Bible Encyclopedia supports this translation: "Primarily, it (iniquity) denotes not an action, but the character of an action, and is so distinguished from sin."[14] Regretfully, many translations, except for the KJV, translate the words to include all manner of sins, including overt sins.

Although all three words are related, they are not the same. The word "avon" (or some form thereof) refers to specific sins like envy or jealousy, and was the word most often used by Job. He used this word in an attempt to get us to name the specific sin of which he was accused.

On the other hand, because we had no knowledge of any actual sins, we preferred to make generalized allegations of evil, or wickedness, or unrighteousness, and so we used the words "aven" or "avel" (or some form thereof).

Whether the words used, describe a general wickedness common to all those born of a woman, or the specific sins of an individual's heart; the focus of the following passages is not on overt sins, but on the extent of the sinfulness of people's nature. These are passages in which the KJV translates the three root words (or some form thereof) as iniquities.

Job 4:7,8. As previously noted, I was encumbered by the fact that I had no knowledge of any specific sins that Job may have committed. Nonetheless, there were two religious tenets of which I was sure. They were:
1. All those born of a woman are evil, vile, and corrupt, and
2. God punishes all those who are evil.

Because of what I believed, I asked the following questions. *Who being innocent ever perished? And when were the righteous ever destroyed? As I see it, those who cultivate iniquity (aven), i.e. wickedness within their heart, and plant trouble, will harvest the same.* Put another way, evil comes to those who are evil, and trouble comes to those who make trouble. The point I was trying to make was: the evil you are experiencing, is because you are evil; and the trouble you are experiencing, is because you are a troublemaker.

Job 5:12,16. I had argued that because Job was born of a woman he had an inherently sinful nature, and therefore it was a certainty he would sin. Further, unless the evil deeds were confessed, God would punish with suffering those who sinned. I believed that the purpose of punishment was to inhibit one's sinful nature, and to discourage the desire to sin. So I said: *God disappoints the schemes of the crafty,* (referring to the hidden sins of the mind) *so that their hands cannot perform* *their enterprise,* (referring to their overt sins). *He snares the wise in their own craftiness, and He smashes headlong the counsel of the willfully stubborn. As a result, they meet with darkness, i.e., they despair, even though light, i.e., hope is available. They grope blindly like those who walk in the darkness of the night. Accordingly, the needy are spared from their slander and from the clutches of the powerful; the poor have hope, and iniquity (avel) i.e., evil, stops her mouth.*

What I meant was; God thwarts the schemes of the crafty, such that the wickedness within the hearts of these people is stopped from expressing itself. The result will be that the poor and the needy have hope. Although this statement was obviously intended for Job, I spoke as if I was speaking of evil people generally, and the message was: the purpose of punishing the wicked with suffering, is to deter the very sins that you are asking us to identify.

Job 6:28-30. Job had rightly accused us of being afraid to acknowledge his righteousness. To do so would mean that God was punishing an innocent man, which we believed was sacrilege. Even to allow for such a possibility would expose us to God's punishment. Therefore, it was important for us to convince him, that he was the cause of his suffering. Relying only on our religious beliefs, we accused him of being an evil and corrupt person.

He counters by saying: *Look at me. Wouldn't it be obvious to you if I were lying? Please take it back. Do not let your iniquity (avel) i.e., your wickedness, stop you. Again, please take your falsehoods back, because my integrity is at stake. Is there anything I said that would disclose to you an iniquity (avel) i.e., an evil, within me?*

Job 7:17,20,21. In addressing God, Job states: *What is man that you should magnify him, and that you should set your heart upon him? If I have sinned, what have I done to you, O preserver of people? Why set me as a mark against you, so that I am a burden to myself? Why don't you simply pardon my* *transgression, and cast away my iniquity (avon) i.e. the sins of my heart?*

Job had consistently asserted his righteousness, and he was particularly upset by the suggestion that God was punishing him because he was born with a corrupt nature. If that were true, then why would God hold people in such high esteem, and why would He set his heart on them?

Also his words: "if I have sinned, what have I done to you," underscore his contention that he had always been obedient. Therefore, why would God (the preserver of people) set him up for punishment, by making him bear a burden of sin and quilt arising out of his human nature? Does He intend to punish him (set him up as a mark) for something he was born with? If God intended to punish him for something he could do nothing about, then why would God require his obedience, and what would be the point in seeking God's approval? Given that God loved him, and given that he had always been obedient, why would God not pardon any overt transgressions that he may have committed, and cast away his iniquities?

Job 10:2-18. In this passage, Job is telling us what he would like to say to God, if only he could find Him. *I will say to God, why do you condemn me? Show me why you oppose me. Does it please you to oppress and despise the work of your own hands, while you smile on the wicked? Do you have the eyes of a human? Do you see as these men see, such that you inquire after my iniquity (avon), i.e., my sins of the heart, and search after my overt sins? If you do, then even though you know that I am innocent, who can deliver me from your hand? Remember, O God, it was you who fashioned me and made me. Would you now destroy what your hands have made? You guided my conception, and formed me in the womb. You clothed me with skin and flesh, and you knit my bones and sinews together. You gave me life, preserved my spirit, and showed me your kindness. I knew that if I sinned, you would be watching me, and would not let my iniquities (avon) i.e., the hidden sins of the heart go unpunished.*

But if I am being punished because of how I was fashioned then why did you bring me out of the womb?

Job spent almost the whole of chapter nine expressing his belief that God created, and controls everything in the universe. In chapter ten he personalizes this belief, and asserts that he is also the product of God's hand. If he were made in such a way that there was a certainty that he would sin, then why would God condemn him, given that God made him?

Furthermore, my friends and I had, without any evidence, quickly arrived at the conclusion, that Job's suffering was punishment for sins that inevitably arose from his sinful nature. Job wants to know if God would also inquire about the hidden sins of his heart, and search for his non-existing overt sins. And why would God do that? It was after all God who had fashioned and made him. If God was punishing him for a sinful nature he was born with, then what would be the point of obedience, and why did God bring him out of the womb in the first place?

Job 11:4,11-14. In this passage Zophar is accusing Job of having an excessively high opinion of himself. He states: *You say to God that your beliefs are flawless and that you are pure in His sight. Well, let me tell you, God knows vain men, and sees their evil deeds as well. Even though you were born as stubborn as a wild ass's colt, a vain man like you would be wise to prepare your heart by stretching out your hands in prayer, putting away your iniquity (avel) i.e., your wickedness, and refusing to allow wrongdoing to dwell in your tent.*

Job 13:23,26. Job is once again expressing what he would like to ask God, if only God would stop punishing and frightening him. *How many are my iniquities (avon) i.e., the specific sins of my heart, and show me what they are? If you consider a windblown leaf like me your enemy because I was born with a sinful nature, then you write down bitter things against me, and you make me inherit the iniquities (avon) i.e., the hidden sins, of my youth.* Note, the words "you write down bitter things against me" is an idiomatic way of saying that you have sentenced me because of my sinful nature, and you make me inherit the iniquities of my youth.

Job knew that he was a righteous man. Nonetheless, we had categorically stated that his suffering was punishment for his sins that arose because he was wicked by nature. So Job decided to turn the matter over to God. He wanted to know specifically what his hidden sins were, and the overt sins that resulted from them. So he postulates that if we were correct, then God must be sentencing him for the hidden sins, harbored in his heart, when he was a youth.

Job 14:17. *My transgressions will be sealed up in a bag, and you will sew up my iniquity (avon) i.e., the sins of my heart.* Job's words cannot be understood apart from the context. His argument is: if he is being punished for sins arising out of his nature then there is more hope for a tree than for him. It also suffers when it is cut down, but it will sprout again. Its roots remain alive and at the scent of water, it will grow again.

He then pleads with God to treat him like a tree. Lay me dormant in the grave for a while, and conceal me until the time allotted to my suffering is passed. Then at least I would have hope, because during the course of my suffering I would know that some day I would be renewed. And then you will call me and I will answer you. You will desire me, the creature your hands have made. Then, if I have sinned, you will not keep track of my offenses. Instead you will seal up my transgressions in a bag (referring to any overt sins that he might have committed) and sew up my iniquity, i.e. the hidden sin of my heart.

Job 15:4-6. Job had persistently demanded that we show him in what way he had sinned. I had no evidence of any overt sin that Job may have committed, so I responded by saying: *your mouth discloses your iniquity (avon) i.e., the sins of your heart, which is a lack of piety and devotion to God. You* *choose the tongue of the crafty. Your own mouth condemns you, not mine: your own lips testify against you.*

Job 15:14-16. Although Job acknowledged the presence of a sinful nature, he consistently denied any specific sins related to it. At the time, I believed his denial was pure nonsense. It was not possible for him to overcome his sinful nature, and I decided to make that clear to him. *What is man that he could be pure, or one born of a woman, that he could be righteous? If God places no trust in his holy ones, and if even the heavens are not pure in his eyes, how much less man, who is vile, and corrupt, and who drinks up iniquity (avel) i.e., evil, like water?*

Job 20:27. Zophar is exasperated by Job's demand to specifically name the sins of his heart. He understands that hidden sins are hard to identify, so in frustration he blurts out that *the heavens will reveal your iniquities (avon) i.e., the specific sins that you are asking us to identify.*

Job 21:19. In one of my earlier speeches, I left the impression that the wicked man's punishment is sometimes exacted on his children. Job is reacting to that statement. *You say that God will punish the children for the iniquities (avon) i.e., the sins of the fathers. But I ask, what good is that? God should punish those who are evil so that they may understand his judgment.* The sins of the fathers referred to here, are sins of the heart, such as deceitful or dishonest nature.

Job 22:5. In this passage I asked a rhetorical question, the answer to which I thought at that time was self-evident. *Are not your transgressions, i.e. your sinful deeds great, and your iniquities, i.e. the sins of your heart infinite?* I was convinced that the nature of all those born of a woman, (which of course included Job's nature,) was corrupt, and that it was a certainty that he had sinned, whether he admitted it or not. I then continued by accusing him of a number of specific sins that I should have known to be untrue. When I now look back, I acknowledge that this marked the low point in our debate, and I am deeply ashamed of what I said.

Job 22:23. It was important for me to point out that if Job wanted to be restored, it would be incumbent upon him to acknowledge, not just those sins that could be seen, but also those that could not. *If you return to the Almighty, you will be restored: if you remove iniquity (evel), i.e., evil, from your heart, then your wealth will be regained and you will find delight in the Almighty.*

A Strange Punishment

In his final address, Job asks the following questions: *What is man's lot from God above, and what is his inheritance from the Almighty? Is it destruction to the wicked, and a strange punishment to the workers of iniquity (aven)?*[15] As we have seen "aven" is a general description of the wickedness within the hearts of all those born of a woman.

Job is reacting to what I said. In my very first speech, I argued that evil does not spring from the soil. It comes from within. We are all born evildoers: i.e., we are all born "workers of iniquity", and therefore, are subject to God's punishment, not only for what we do, but also for who we are.

Job acknowledged that people have a sinful nature when he declares: "Who can bring what is pure from the impure? No one!"[16] But he insists that mankind has already been punished. Specifically he states: "Man born of a woman is of few days, and full of trouble. ... He springs up like a flower, and withers away: like a fleeting shadow, he does not endure. ... Man's days are determined. (God has) decreed the number of his months, and (has) set limits he cannot exceed."[17] Job then inquires of God: "Do you fix your eye on such a one? Will you bring him before you for judgment?"[18] Put another way: will you punish him again for the same offense, for which he has already been punished?

Already in a previous speech, Job had questioned God. "Why hast thou set me as a mark against thee, so that I am a burden to myself?"[19] In other words: why do you set me up for punishment, by using the nature I was born with, against me? Job resents being punished for something that was not of his doing, and that he could do nothing about.

He then argues that our position leads to a life of futility. He states: "Since I am already found guilty, why should I struggle in vain? Even if I washed myself with soap, and my hands with washing soda, (God) would still plunge me into a slime pit."[20]

Job had effectively pointed out that, if what we said were true; then he was subject to double jeopardy. He was being punished a second time for the offense of being who he was when he was born, i.e., a worker of iniquity. Therefore, as he concludes his defense he asks: Is this really man's lot from God? Is it destruction to those who do evil, and the strange punishment of double jeopardy to those born a worker of iniquity?

Wisdom

Finally we are left with just one more question. Why did Job choose to begin his last speech with a discourse on wisdom and understanding?

My friends and I began our speeches by accusing Job of lacking wisdom and understanding in respect to the cause of his suffering. We alleged that his tribulations arose because he was born of a woman. In my first speech, I shared with Job what I had learned from personal observation, and what had been revealed to me in a vision.[21] In my second and third speech I shared what I had learned from wise men, my own experience, and from logic.[22] Bildad relied on ancestral wisdom and tradition. Zophar relied on history.[23] But what cannot be denied, is that we all relied on our theology. All of the authorities and support that we relied on was for the purpose of buttressing our preconceived religious views.

Job wishes to discredit our claim to wisdom and understanding, and our assertion that we had found wisdom in various authorities such as visions, ancestors, wise men, history, experience or logic. He states, that although wisdom and understanding are more valuable than all the treasures in the world, they cannot be found by people. (He was of course referring to us.) But God had found these invaluable treasures: to revere God – that is wisdom, and to shun evil – that is understanding.

Reverence for God is an attitude or attribute, not an act. Hence it goes to character, not conduct. In other words, Job is saying that wisdom is found in those whose character is to revere God, and whose conduct is to shun evil. This of course, is precisely what he claimed for himself.

Two things should be noted.
1. Although Job could not have known it, God described him in much the same way when He said to Satan: have you considered my servant Job? He is a man of blameless conduct and an upright nature, "a man who fears God and shuns evil."[24]
2. Nonetheless, God was unhappy that Job had claimed wisdom and understanding for himself. In fact, when God eventually addressed Job, He found it necessary to remind him that it was He, "who endows the heart with wisdom (and) gives understanding to the mind."[25]

CHAPTER 6

GOD'S RESPONSE

It was obvious to us that Job was suffering terribly. Every day brought to view another aspect of his severe suffering. He suffered physically, mentally and emotionally. He suffered derision, scorn, isolation and ridicule. He suffered the death of his large family, and the love and enjoyment they brought him. He suffered the loss of his possessions, and the security, prestige, and power that wealth can bring. He suffered the loss of his friends and acquaintances, leaving him feeling rejected and alone. A painful and debilitating disease ravished his body. Whatever pain, agony, grief and distress people suffer, likely found a home in him.

The underlying question for all parties was: why was he suffering like this? My friends and I were convinced that God was punishing him because he had sinned, and therefore he was the cause of his own suffering. Job insisted that he had not sinned, but that for reasons he did not understand, God was causing him to suffer, and he wanted to know why.

God's fascinating and astonishing response (which fully answers Job's question) consists of three parts, each disclosing a different aspect of His universe. They are:

a. The marvels and mysteries of the inanimate world, (38:4-38)

b. The marvels and mysteries of the animate world (38:39-39:30), and

c. The marvels and mysteries of the spiritual world. (40:9-41:34)

There are two consistent themes that are woven through the three parts of His reply. The themes are: (1) a reset of Job's relationship with God, and (2) a demonstration that He is the Sovereign Creator of the universe. The implications of this statement will be explored in the next chapter.

Apart from the common themes, each part of God's response also has its own purpose, and will be dealt with next.

I. Part One (38:1-38)

Throughout the debate, Job had, in a somewhat belligerent tone, persistently and aggressively challenged God. When addressing God directly, he sarcastically and bitterly queries; "Does it please you to oppress me, to spurn the works of your hands, while you smile on the schemes of the wicked? ... Withdraw your hand far from me, and stop frightening me with your terrors. Then summon me and I will answer, or let me speak, and you reply. How many wrongs and sins have I committed? Show me my offense and my sin. Why do you hide your face...?"[1] Later he complains about God's lack of justice when he alleges: "know that God has wronged me.... Though I cry, 'I've been wronged!' I get no response; though I call for help, there is no justice."[2] He argues that if God would listen then, "I would state my case before Him, and fill my mouth with arguments. I would find out what He would answer me, and consider what He would say."[3]

God's response indicates that He considered Job's relationship with Him to be the most important. The rest could wait. His first words are intended to reset the parameters of their relationship, both in respect to Job's attitude, and his accusations. "Who is this that darkens my counsel with words without wisdom? ... I will question you, and you shall answer me."[4]

God then takes Job on a virtual cosmic tour, and throughout the tour God asks him a number of question. One of the reasons for the questions was to highlight Job's limited understanding, as compared with God's infinite knowledge.

For example, as they were touring the inanimate part of the universe, God asked the following. Tell me Job, where were you when I made the earth; and who do you think designed it? Do you understand for what purpose it was created? Who do you think held back the seas as they were being formed? Were you there when I fixed its boundaries?

Have you ever gone to the bottom of the ocean, or walked in the deepest caves? Do you know everything there is to know about the expanses of the earth? Tell me if you know all this.

What is the source of light and darkness? You must have learned something given that you have already lived for many years. Have you ever been to the north or south poles, or to the skies where hail is formed? Do you have any idea what creates lightning, or what motivates the trade winds, or why thunderstorms take the path they do? Do you understand how these things happen, or why they happen? Do you know how ice is formed, and why it becomes hard as stone?

Who do you think holds the universe together, and has the wisdom to count the clouds? Do you know why the constellations appear in the same place each season? Do you understand the laws that govern the heavens and the earth? And even if you did, who gives wisdom to the heart, and understanding to the mind?

God then tours Job through his animate world and continues to ask a number of questions. (The individual questions will be dealt with next, in part two of God's response.)

By the time this second part of the tour was over, Job was ready to acknowledge his inappropriate attitude, and the inequality of the relationship. He states: "I am unworthy – how can I reply to you? I put my hand over my mouth. I spoke once, but I have no answer – twice, but I will say not more."[5]

But God was not yet done. Job had accused God of doing Him wrong. He had alleged that God was unjust because He had punished a righteous man. Consequently, God takes this opportunity to ask: "Will the one who contends with the

Almighty correct Him? Let him who accuses God answer Him. ... I will question you, and you shall answer me. Would you discredit my justice? Would you condemn me to justify yourself?"[6]

Then came the tour through the spiritual world, but before the tour began, God reestablishes the rules of engagement. He instructs Job: "brace yourself like a man; I will question you and you shall answer me."[7]

(What Job saw, and what God asked will be dealt with in part three of God's answer.) Suffice it to say that Job had learned his lesson: the parties to this relationship are not equal. One is the creator: the other the created. One the potter: the other the clay. One is infinite: the other is finite. One is omnipotent and omniscient: the other is powerless and ignorant by comparison. One was to question: the other was to answer. One is to be worshipped: the other is to worship.

This time Job's expression of regret was complete. He acknowledges the impropriety of his accusations, the inequality of their relationship, and the need to adjust his attitude. He admits: "I know that you can do all things; no plan of yours can be thwarted. You asked, 'Who is this that obscures my counsel without knowledge?' Surely I spoke of things I did not understand, things too wonderful for me to know. You said, 'Listen now, and I will speak; I will question you, and you will answer me.' My ears had heard of you but now my eyes have seen you. Therefore I despise myself and repent in dust and ashes."[8]

But there was still one lesson to be learned. Job had acknowledged that even though many items on earth and in the universe testify of the power of God: He himself, could not be found. Throughout the debate, Job repeated this complaint because he wanted to personally ask God: Why are you doing this to me?

God responds by referencing the same items that Job had referenced.[9] He says in effect: really Job, you say that you cannot see me. But can you not see me in the world that I created? You acknowledged that I am the creator of the sun, stars and sea. Can you not see me in these items? Are you willfully blind? What God was trying to teach Job, was what King David later learned when he exclaimed, "the heavens declare the glory of God: the skies proclaim the works of His hand. Day after day they pour forth speech; night after night they display knowledge. There is no speech or language where their voice is not heard. Their voice goes out into all the earth, their words to the ends of the world."[10]

II. Part Two (38:38-40:14)

As previously noted, in the second part of His response, God continues the tour of the animate part of his universe to demonstrate the inequality of their relationship.

However, God's principle purpose in "part two," was to teach us something about the issue of suffering and hardship. His response directly contradicted what we all believed to be true. Job was convinced that God was punishing him with suffering, but he did not know why. We had argued that Job was suffering because he was born with a sinful nature, and therefore he had unquestionably sinned. Now God is vindicating and comforting Job by assuring him that he was not the cause of his own bodily suffering. Instead, suffering arises out of, and is a part of nature, and has no morality attached to it. We have since learned that in Job's case it arose from a disease inflicted upon him, but generally speaking, bodily suffering is the body's natural response to the abnormal.

Suffering and hardship are what Job was referring to when he said: "Man born of a woman is of few days and full of trouble."[11] Suffering (like death) was the result of God's curse for Adam's original sin,[12] but it is now a part of nature, and is not personal.

Stripped from personal morality, suffering is nothing more than pain, distress or severe hardship experienced by all living creatures. Birds and animals also suffer, but they do not sin. Therefore, it cannot be said that their suffering is punishment for any personal wrongdoing.

To demonstrate this point, God asks Job to take a close look at the animate part of nature, and particularly the individual characteristics of some of the birds and animals that inhabit His creation. All of the creatures that God used as examples lived in the region, and hence we knew their distinguishing characteristics. As a result, in His response, God was brief and direct. For your benefit however, I will add some background information (in parenthesis) that is implicit in God's response.

He begins by directing Job's attention to the lioness and her cubs, and then asks: do you hunt the prey for the lioness or satisfy the hunger of her cubs as they crouch in their dens or in a nearby thicket and wait? [13]

(The cubs depend entirely on the lioness for food, so when she hunts, they must crouch in their den, and wait for her to return. It is at this time that the cubs are most vulnerable. Some of her cubs will likely die of starvation, either because the lioness was unable to provide food, or because she was injured in obtaining it. I alluded to the lion's vulnerability when, in comparing Job's diminished status to the lioness, I said: "the lion perishes for lack of prey, and the cubs of the lioness are scattered."[14] As she gets older, her task becomes even more difficult and eventually she too will die of starvation. Even King David makes reference to the lions' desperate struggle for food: "the lions roar for their prey, but seek their food from God."[15]

Against this background, God is effectively asking: you want me to alleviate your suffering, but do you hunt the prey for the lioness, and mitigate the hunger pains of her newborn cubs? Are the hardships of the lioness in obtaining the prey, and hunger pains of the cubs the result of my punishment?)

But perhaps hunting on behalf of the lioness is too dangerous for you Job, so what about the ravens? Who provides the food for the raven when its young cry out to God, and wander about for lack of food?

(I do not know why there would have been a lack of food for fledging ravens. Whatever the reason, God makes reference to this deprivation in His response. King David also observes: "God provides food for the young ravens when they call."[16] Jesus asks His disciples to "consider the ravens: they do not sow or reap, they have no storehouse or barn; yet God feeds them."[17] What I do know, is that the pain of starvation has been described as one of the most severe, and cries out for satisfaction.)

Do you want to talk about pain, suffering, or hardship, Job? "Do you know when the mountain goat gives birth?"[18] Of course you don't because they live, and give birth on steep and dangerous cliffs, and as such are virtually inaccessible.[19]

So what about the common deer? Do you watch when the doe painfully bears her fawn? Do you count the months till they bear? Do you know the time they give birth? You don't know that either do you Job, because to protect her fawn from the rain and wind, and to avoid predators, she gives birth in secret places. Even then, she will simply crouch down and bring forth her young; and only then would her labor pains end. Nonetheless, her young will thrive and grow strong in the wild. Eventually they will leave and do not return.

(There are at least two factors that we should bear in mind as we consider this passage. First: the pain that any female experiences during the birthing process can be extremely painful. The KJV describes the process of the doe giving birth as: "they cast out their sorrows."[20] The HCSB translates this passage to say: "have you watched the deer in labor?" In fact, under the heading of "pain", almost all dictionaries have a separate category for labor pain.[21] Second: King David alludes to the secretive nature of the doe when she gives birth. He states: "the voice of the Lord made the hinds (i.e., young female deer) to calf."[22] The deer is the prey for all the large predators, and as a result, they live their entire lives in fear and apprehension. And yet, even under these circumstances they give birth, and the young thrive, grow strong, and leave.)

God next points to the wild donkey and inquires: Who freed this animal? Who untied his ropes? This animal has an indomitable spirit, and a desire to be isolated and free. So I gave him the wasteland as his home, and the salt flats as his habitat. Do you know anything about the hardship the wild donkey experiences as he attempts to sustain himself? He ranges the hills for his pasture, and searches for any green thing. But you already knew that, didn't you Job. In explaining why you were complaining you asked; "Does a wild donkey bray when it has grass?"[23] You knew that they bray only to express their severe hunger, but when they are well fed they don't bray at all. You said that, because you wanted your friends to know that you had something to complain about. In fact, you know all about the hardships these animals endure. It was you who said: "like wild donkeys in the wilderness, the poor must spend all their time searching, even in the desert, for food for their children."[24] Do you think that these animals are suffering because they are being punished? If so, for what? So why do you think that your suffering is punishment?

(The hardship and suffering of the wild donkey was well known and is vividly pictured in Jeremiah: "Wild donkeys stand on the barren heights and pant like jackals; their eyesight fails for lack of pasture."[25] The lesson to be learned is that hardships and suffering are simply a part of nature.)

The next example is that of the wild ox. Will the wild ox consent to serve you? Will he stay by your manger at night? Can you hold him to the furrow with a harness? Will he till the valleys behind you? Will you rely on him for his great strength? Will you leave your heavy work to him? Can you trust him to bring in your grain, and gather it to your threshing floor?

(This was an animal of great strength that could not be controlled. Yet despite its strength and independent spirit, it is now extinct. It is not clear what caused it to become extinct, but obviously as a species, it was unable to overcome its hardships.

The next three examples demonstrate that even birds and animals do not "will" foreseeable harm. Whatever harm arises may be a consequence of their nature, but they do not seek it either for themselves or for another. This part of God's answer was made necessary because all the participants to the debate believed, that inasmuch as God was sovereign, He must have "willed" Job's suffering.[26] As previously noted, we disagreed only as to why.)

The ostrich joyfully flaps her wings. She has feathers, but she cannot fly. She lays her eggs on the ground, and lets them warm in the sand; unmindful that a foot may crush them, or that some wild animal may trample them. She treats her young harshly, as if they were not hers; she cares not that her labor was in vain, for God did not endow her with wisdom, or give her a share of good sense. Yet, when she spreads her feathers to run, she laughs at horse and rider.

(It has long been accepted, that in relation to its size, the ostrich has the smallest brain in the world. It also has the habit of lowering its head when confronted with danger. It appears that the ostrich believes that when it lowers its head, it makes itself smaller. Also, because of their disregard for their eggs and for their young, they have a reputation of being heartless. This apparent neglect is graphically portrayed in Lamentations 4:3. "Even jackals offer their breasts to nurse their young, but my people have become heartless like ostriches in the desert." The point that God is making is this: if a brainless or heartless ostrich doesn't intend to put her eggs in harms way, why do you suppose that I would intend to harm you?)

Do you give the horse his strength, or clothe his neck with a flowing mane? Did you give him the capacity to leap or to snort so proudly? He is a magnificent creature, with fearless courage, such that even in the presence of imminent and foreseeable danger he charges into battle. In fact he is eager for it. At the blast of the trumpet he snorts, "Aha!" Do you suppose he "wills" to die? When he sees others suffering as they are impaled on a phalanx of swords, he is not deterred because he was created fearless.

(The unwavering nature of this animal is referenced in Jeremiah 8:6. "Like a horse charging into battle, each person pursues his own course." Even though it may cause him great suffering, the horse is what it is, and does what it does, because it was created that way. So Job, tell me, if a magnificent horse does not seek its own foreseeable suffering, under what circumstance would I want you to suffer?)

Does the hawk take flight by your wisdom and spread his wings toward the south? (This is another example of God's infinite sovereign creativity. It is the miracle of migration. But it is also wrought with hazards and hardships. Every year the migrating hawks are overcome by an irresistible urge to migrate, but those too weak, too old, or too young, do not survive. It is thought that almost all migrating birds of any kind, eventually die during the migration. If so, then as the hawk gets older, its urge to migrate will seal its death. And yet it flies, not because it wishes to suffer and die, but because it is a hawk.)

Finally God ends with the example of the eagle. Does the eagle soar at your command, and build his nest on high? He dwells on a cliff, and stays there at night; a rocky crag is his home. From there he seeks out the food that his eyes detect from afar. His young feast on blood, and where the slain are, there is he.

(The eagle is often referenced in the Bible as the epitome of perfection, grace and glory. In Proverbs, King Solomon exclaims: "There are three things that are too amazing for me, four that I do not understand, (and one is) the way of the eagle in the sky."[27]

And yet consider the miserable hardships experienced by these magnificent birds. They dwell on cold, windy and dangerous cliffs – even at night. They have no protection from the rain. From there they seek out their food, and feed their young the flesh and blood of decomposing animals. What God is pointing out, is that these majestic birds experience hardships, and sustain their young with spoiled meat, but not as punishment for sin.)

God began His examples with the lion – the king of the beasts, and He ends with the eagle – the queen of the birds. In evaluating this part of God's response, I note that He had at least three purposes. They were:
1. To demonstrate His sovereign wisdom, imagination, power and creativity through the creatures that He had created.
2. To demonstrate Job's limited understanding of even those birds and animals that he was familiar with.
3. To demonstrate that suffering is not punishment and does not arise from God's will to punish, but is simply a part of nature.

It should be noted that at no time did God give Job a scientific explanation for his suffering, because the point was not what caused it, but what didn't. Job's suffering was not the consequence of his own sin, as we thought. Nor was it God's punishment for reasons unknown, as Job thought.

III. Part Three (40:14-41:34)

A. The Behemoth and the Leviathan
(This part of God's response requires some analysis. God directs Job's attention to various evil forces that in our time were known as the "Behemoth" and the "Leviathan."[28] They were part of the mythology and culture where we lived. The evil forces were pictured as having animal bodies with human personalities and characteristics.)

God uses these same images in describing the evil forces when He states: look at the Behemoth that I made when I made man. He has great strength and influence, and is capable of great destruction. He ranks first among the works of God, yet now I must approach him with my sword. He lives comfortably on the earth, and is often concealed or camouflaged. He is not afraid of the power of nature, and he cannot be captured and controlled by man.

(This is the only place in the Bible where the word: "Behemoth" is used. Because it was described as first in rank among the works of God (NIV), it is likely the same Satan who appeared to Adam and Eve in the form of a serpent. Having been thrown out of heaven, this evil creature now makes earth his home.]

God then tells Job something about the second evil creature that He also has to contend with. Can you capture or control the Leviathan? Will he beg you for mercy, or speak gently to you? Will he agree to serve you? Can you put him on a leash for your little girls to play with? Can you cause him to suffer? If you lay a hand on him, you will remember the struggle, and never do it again. Any hope of subduing him is false. He is a creature that cannot be captured, controlled or conquered by man. He is not someone that you want to make an agreement with. He is powerful, and it is better to flee from him. He is heartless, fearsome and deceptive. He can be both attractive and revolting. He can hold himself out as the source of wisdom and security, but only dismay and disappointment result.

Who, but me, can approach and control him? He is invincible to you. He can be intimidating and terrifying. There is nothing like him on earth – he is a creature without fear. He looks down on all that are haughty, and he is the king over all that are proud. So Job, if you cannot stand against the Leviathan, can you stand against me, or make a claim that I must pay? Everything under heaven already belongs to me.

(It is likely that the Leviathan represents the same evil force as the Behemoth, but in a different form. It is interesting to note, that when God describes His interaction with the evil force, He calls it the Behemoth. However, when He describes man's interaction with the same evil force, He refers to it as the Leviathan.

That Job was well aware of these creatures is evidenced by the fact that he had also referred to the Leviathan. Already, in his opening speech, he was bemoaning his birth. He regretted not just the day he was born, but wished that the date had not even existed on the calendar. He then suggests: may those who curse days (i.e., the sorcerers) call on the Leviathan, and curse that day.[29])

B. The issue of evil

And this brings us to the essence of part three of God's answer, in which He addresses the issue of evil. My friends and I had insisted, that despite his denials, Job must have sinned because he was born of a woman, i.e. because of his sinful human nature. We described mankind as follows. "What is man that he could be pure, or one born of a women that he could be righteous? ... Man is vile and corrupt, who drinks up evil like water. Humans are maggots and worms. They conceive trouble, give birth to evil, and their womb fashions deceit. They remain in bondage to their cravings, and they cannot save themselves."[30]

When Job continued to insist that he was blameless, we accused him of being dishonest, crafty and a hypocrite. I now recognize that this was said to the face of a man whom God had described as "blameless and upright, a man who fears God and shuns evil." I feel ashamed as I think of it.

So God decides to set the record straight. The original source of evil was not the heart of man. The source was outside of man in what God describes as the Behemoth and the Leviathan.

Elsewhere in Scripture, many other names are used to identify the evil forces. Isaiah identifies the Leviathan as a fallen angel,[31] and King David describes the consequences of his fall when he states: "It was (God) who crushed the heads of the Leviathan."[32] The word "heads" suggests that the Leviathan had followers. The fact that their heads were crushed, may mean that their capacity to think up evil schemes was diminished.

From *The Book of Revelation* we learn how these evil forces, (now called the great dragon, or the ancient serpent), came to dwell on earth. "Then there was war in heaven. Michael and his angels fought against the dragon and his angels. The dragon lost the battle, and he and his angels were forced out of heaven. This great dragon – the ancient serpent called the devil, or Satan, the one deceiving the whole world – was thrown down to the earth with all his angels. ... Terror will come on the earth and the sea, for the devil has come down to you in great anger, knowing that he has little time."[33]

Although we do not know much about the origins of the Leviathan, we do know how his war with God will end. Isaiah tells us that in the final Day of Judgment, "the Lord will punish with his sword ... the Leviathan, the gliding or coiling serpent; He will slay the monster of the sea."[34]

In the meantime evil, i.e. the Leviathan, lives on earth and God's struggle with him continues. *The Book of Revelation*, describes an epic battle between God, and the Leviathan for the control of the earth.[35] Because the authority to govern this earth was given to man, the heart of man is both the prize and the arena in which the battle is fought.

In fact, we are urged to be participants with God in this fight. The apostle Paul encourages all Christians to "put on the full armor of God, so that you can take your stand against the devil's schemes. For your struggle is not against flesh and blood, but ... against the powers of the dark world, and against the spiritual forces of evil in the heavenly realms."[36]

C. The sin of pride

God concludes by saying: "There is nothing on earth like him; he is a creature without fear. He looks down on all that are haughty; he is king over all that are proud."[37] What God is pointing out, is that for some people the Leviathan is king. They are the haughty and proud. This may have been a warning to Job. We had accused him of being arrogant, and given that he wanted to "contend with the Almighty (to) correct him,"[38] I believe we may have been right.

In Proverbs the seven deadly sins are listed and pride comes first.[39] Pride is an unduly high opinion of oneself. For the proud there is no need for God.

It was pride that had Satan (the Leviathan) evicted from heaven. In Isaiah we read: "you (Satan) have been cast down to the earth (because) you said in your heart, I will make myself like the Most High."[40] Ezekiel more fully describes his eviction; "you were blameless in your ways, from the day you were created till wickedness was found in you. So I drove you in disgrace from the mount of God ... (because) your heart became proud."[41] It was pride that caused Adam and Eve to sin. They succumbed to Satan's temptation when he said; "For God knows that when you eat of the fruit of the tree of life, and of the knowledge of good and evil, your eyes will be opened, and you will be like God."[42]

The intransigent nature of pride was disclosed to Job when God said: if you have the power or influence to "look at every proud man and humble him ... then I will admit to you that your own right hand can save you."[43]

CHAPTER 7

EPILOGUE

A. Introduction

This brings us back to where we started. Although God was unhappy with Job, He was outright angry with us. After God spoke to Job, he turned to me and said: *"I am angry with you and your two friends, because you have not spoken of me what is right as my servant Job has. So now take seven bulls and seven rams and go to my servant Job and sacrifice a burnt offering for yourselves. My servant Job will pray for you, and I will accept his prayer and not deal with you according to your folly. You have not spoken of me what is right as my servant Job has."*[1]

God had in effect accused us of slander. Twice He said that we had not spoken right about Him, but why would that be?

B. The Criteria to be met

Without doubt God's message is lost if the reader does not understand why God was angry with us. That is particularly true given that we believed that we were speaking highly of God. So what was it we said that was so offensive? When considering God's reprimand, I note that the offensive statements consisted of the following characteristics.

1. They were statements that were disparaging of God. This is clear from the words: "I am angry with you because you have not spoken of <u>me what is right</u>...." We had said many derogatory and hurtful things about Job. However, what was said about Job was not what made God angry. God did not say, "You have not spoken about Job what is right." Rather He said: "you have not spoken of <u>me</u> what is right as my servant Job has."

2. They were statements that were not only disparaging of God, but were also false. God was angry because we had not spoken of Him, "<u>what is right</u>."
3. They were statements that were different from any statements that Job had made. God had accused us of not speaking of Him what was right "<u>as my servant Job has</u>."
4. They were statements made by us that were false, while the corresponding statements made by Job on the same subject matter were true. God's accusation against us was: "<u>You have not spoken of me what is right, as my servant Job has</u>." If what Job said was wrong, (even if for different reasons) then the statements made by us on the topic in question, were not the statements that God found offensive.
5. They were statements that were so offensive, as to cause God to require my friends and me, to atone for our sin of slander by way of a sacrifice.

C. What were our offensive statements?

What offended God was our combined assertion that those whom He had so carefully created were already in the womb totally evil, despicable and corrupt. It is in their nature to be so. They conceive sin, their womb fashions deceit, and they give birth to evildoers who drink up evil like water. They do so because evil is sweet and they crave it. They were unable to save themselves from their cravings. Their nature is such that as surely as sparks fly up from a fire, they will sin. All people are but maggots and worms.

We knew Job to be a good and righteous man. Nonetheless, I admit that we did our best to impugn both his character and his conduct. All three of us eventually accused him of actually sinning. Our accusations were based, not on what we knew about him, but on what we believed to be true. We believed that everyone born of a woman had a sinful nature, and therefore it was inevitable that they would sin. We were so convinced of our religious beliefs that we were prepared to contradict what we knew to be true. To our shame, I will briefly summarize my speeches, and then those of my friends.

Summary of my arguments

In my very first speech I state in effect: My experience shows that those who plant trouble and cultivate evil will harvest the same. (The implication was: if Job was experiencing evil and trouble, in the form of suffering and loss, it was because he was an evildoer and a troublemaker.) Evil does not spring from the soil nor does trouble sprout from the ground. It comes from within. All people are born evildoers, and as such they will do evil just as surely as sparks fly upwards from a fire.[2]

In my second speech, I elaborate on man's sinful nature. What is mankind that he could be pure, or one born of a woman that he could be righteous? If God places no trust in the holy ones, if even the heavens are not pure in His eyes, how much less man, who is vile and corrupt, and who drinks up evil like water. All people are wicked. They conceive trouble and give birth to evil. Their womb fashions deceit.[3]

In my third and final speech, I give up in frustration. Job had consistently demanded that we specifically identify any sin that he committed, but we were unable to do so. Yet I was so convinced of my theology that I simply accused Job of a number of sins.[4] I did so knowing that Job had a reputation as a good and righteous man, and I had no evidence to support my accusations. As between Job, as I knew him, and my religious beliefs, as I understood them; I chose my religious beliefs.

Summary of Bildad's arguments

In his first speech, Bildad picks up on what I said about the sinfulness of human nature. In particular, he believes that because all people are born evildoers, there is a certainty that all will sin. This forms the basis of his accusation that: "your children must have sinned, so their punishment was well deserved."⁵ He is not bothered by the fact that he had no evidence of any actual sins. He also relies on his religious belief; i.e., because of their sinful nature, the children must have sinned.

In his second speech, he forthrightly accuses Job of wickedness. He, like myself, had no evidence of any actual sins, but as previously noted, he strongly believed that all those born of a woman are inherently evil. Furthermore, God punishes evil people with suffering. He then applies his views to Job, and concludes that all Job's sufferings were because he was wicked.⁶ In other words; Job's suffering was itself confirmation of his sinfulness.

In his final speech, Bildad provides the basis for the allegations that both Job and his children were evil. In essence he states: No one can be righteous before God. How can one born of a woman be pure? If the stars are not pure in his eyes, how much less is man, who is but a maggot, or a son of man, who is only a worm? ⁷

Summary of Zophar's arguments

In his first speech, Zophar claims to know the mind of God. He states, that God knows vain men, (referring to Job's character) and sees their wickedness also (referring to his conduct.)⁸ It did not matter to him whether Job was being punished because of a sinful character, or because of some overt sin. He states that if God chooses to bring judgment against you because of your character, who can hinder Him?⁹ On the other hand, he also believes that because Job was born vile and corrupt, he must have committed some overt sins. He surmises that Job had actually sinned so often, that God had probably forgotten some of them.¹⁰

In his second speech, he describes all people's sinful nature. He states, that for all people, evil is sweet. They hide it under their tongue, and they cannot let it go. They have no respite from their cravings, and they cannot save themselves.[11]

In his final speech, Zophar describes at length, and in detail, the fate of those who do not acknowledge their wickedness. However, he was saddled with the same problem we all had; he had no knowledge of any actual sins. As such, he also relied on his religious belief, that all people sin because they are inherently wicked. Consequently, he begins his description of God's punishments by stating: "Here is the fate God allots to wicked people."[12] Because he cannot point to any particular sin that Job had committed, he is forced to make a generalized allegation of wickedness that he believed to be true of all people.[13]

D. Were our Statements False?

We said that Job could not be righteous, because all those born of a woman were totally evil, vile and corrupt. If that were true, we would all be devils, and all God's enemies deserving of punishment. God himself declared our statements to be false at least twice.

Firstly, we all thought that Job was being punished. The only issue was: why? In addressing God, Job demands to know: "why do you consider me your enemy?" The predominant purpose of part 3 of God's response was to assure Job that he was not an enemy. God does so by describing the real evil adversary. It is the Behemoth, aka, the Leviathan, about whom God said: "on earth there is nothing like him." (Chap. 41:33) What this means, is that; innately, people are nothing like devils, and are not God's enemies.

Secondly, on several occasions God described Job as blameless and upright. What God said about Job should be sufficient to convince anyone that what we said about all people was wrong. However, Job was not the only one to disprove our religious views.

Ezekiel describes Noah and Daniel who, at different times, were just as righteous as Job.[14]

Hebrews 11 refers to Abel as righteous, to Enoch as one who pleased God, and to Abraham as one who obeyed.[15]

Samuel was an honest and God-fearing prophet that, "All Israel recognized ... as the Prophet of the Lord."[16]

Jehoshaphat "sought the Lord with all his heart."[17]

Jotham was a king of Judah, "who did what was right in the eyes of the Lord."[18]

Hezekiah " trusted in the Lord, the God of Israel. There was no one like him among all the kings of Judah, either before or after him. He held fast to the Lord and did not cease to follow Him."[19]

Josiah "did what was right in the eyes of the Lord ... not turning aside to the right or to the left. ... Neither before nor after Josiah was there a king like him who turned to the Lord as he did – with all his heart and with all his soul and with all his strength."[20]

All of these people were born of a woman.

Although we had made a number of false statements that were disparaging of Job, it was not the reason God was angry with us. He was offended because we had not spoken right about Him. The question then is: how were our false statements also disparaging of God?

E. How were our statements disparaging of God?

1. Regarding God as Creator.

The Bible chronicles the creation of man as follows: "Then God said, 'Let us make man in our own image, in our likeness, and let them have dominion over the earth.' And God did so, and He saw all that He had made, and it was very good."[21] In Proverbs, wisdom is personified. When God created the world, "I (wisdom) was the craftsman at God's side. I was filled with delight day after day, rejoicing always in His presence, rejoicing in His whole world and delighting in mankind."[22]

But Adam and Eve fell, and as a consequence of their sin, my friends and I believed that all people became inherently evil, despicable and corrupt.

Job vigorously disagreed. Already during the first round of speeches, when speaking to God, he states: "What is man, that you make so much of him, and that you set your heart on him?" He then makes it personal: "Your hands shaped me and made me ... you molded me like clay ... you guided my conception, and formed me in the womb ... you clothed me with skin and flesh, and knit me together with bones and sinews ... you gave me life and showed me kindness, and in your providence watched over my spirit."[23] He goes so far as to say: "God longs for the creature that his hands have made."[24] In his final address, he relates how he was always respectful of everyone because: "God created both me and my servants. He created us both in the womb."[25]

In Psalm 8, King David relates God's regard for man as he now is: "What is man that you are mindful of him, or the son of man that you care for him? You made him a little lower than the heavenly beings and crowned him with glory and honor."[26] In Psalm 139 he continues: "For you created my inmost being; you knit me together in my mother's womb. I praise you because I am fearfully and wonderfully made; ... I know that full well."[27] Isaiah reminds the Israelites that it was God "who made you and formed you."[28] In Zechariah, God identifies Himself as "the Lord, who stretches out the heavens, who lays the foundation of the earth, and who forms the spirit of man within him."[29] These passages teach that God fashioned the body and mind of every individual, and every birth is the miracle of a new creation.

If people changed from being totally good to totally evil, that change must be attributed to the influence of Satan at the time of the fall. If, as alleged by my friends and me, all people are now addicts of sin, from which they cannot extricate themselves, then Satan (a creature that God created,) has recreated man into his own image. In so doing he has replaced God as man's new creator, and it is he who now "forms the spirit of man within him."

2. Regarding the Providence of God

To refute our accusation that he was inherently evil, Job argued that, not only had God carefully created him, but also that, "you showed me kindness, and in your providence watched over my spirit." What is to be made of God's providence, if on His watch, all those who were so carefully and skillfully molded by Him, are now completely corrupt?

Further, Job refers to God as, "the preserver of man."[30] What reasonable interpretation can be given to the word "preserver," if all people are totally evil and corrupt? What were they preserved from? Or perhaps more important, what are they preserved for?

In Isaiah, God himself describes what He did, and will do. "I have upheld you since you were conceived, and have carried you since your birth. Even to your old age ... I am He who will sustain you. I have made you and I will carry you, ... and rescue you."[31] What possible meaning can be given to God's words if all people conceive sin, if their wombs fashion deceit, and if they give birth to evildoers who drink up evil like water, and who crave it and have no respite from their cravings?

3. Regarding God as Lord.

If what we claimed was true, then not only has Satan replaced God as humanity's Creator, but he has also replaced God as humanity's Lord. After God created Adam and Eve, He mandated them to manage His universe. In Genesis 1, we read: "God blessed them and said to them, 'be fruitful and increase in number; fill the earth and subdue it. Rule over the fish of the sea and the birds of the air and over every living creature that moves on the ground.'"[32]

In other words, God delegated to people the duty and responsibility to manage His creation on His behalf. In fact, people were created for that purpose. In Genesis 2 we learn: "When the Lord made the earth and the heavens ... there was no man to work the ground ... (so) the Lord God formed the man from the dust of the ground and breathed into his nostrils the breath of life, and the man became a living being.... The Lord God took the man and put him in the Garden of Eden to work it and to take care of it."[33]

After Adam fell, God's will in respect to the whole of his creation was the same as for the Garden of Eden. Isaiah states: "God did not create the world to be empty, but formed it to be inhabited."[34] In Psalm 8, King David describes the "inhabitants" delegated right to manage God's creation as follows: "You made him ruler over the works of your hands; you put <u>everything</u> under his feet."[35] The governance and stewardship over all that God created remains the responsibility of all people.

Moreover, because God chose to delegate the right to manage His creation to all people, He did not thereby diminish His authority. Both His capacity to govern and His authority to govern are unlimited. Consequently, when God delegates some of His authority to govern to man, that does not mean that His authority is now diminished to the same extent as man's authority is enhanced. It is not like a glass of water where, if half is given away, then only half remains. God's authority to govern, i.e. His sovereignty was always unlimited. Hence, when He delegated some, what was left was still unlimited.

Also, just as God does not ordinarily interfere in the rules of nature, so too He does not generally interfere in man-made rules arising out of His delegated authority. And herein lies an important point. When those to whom God has delegated His authority do wrong, whether intentionally or otherwise, God does not usually intervene. As a result, much happens that would not have happened if God had retained his direct authority and control. It was God's will to delegate His authority to man, and in so doing, man must now answer to God.

However, if people are as we described, then Satan controls their life, because they are no longer managers responsible to God, but evildoers in bondage to sin, and hence have no capacity to do anything other than sin. The management of God's creation has then been placed under the new management of maggots and worms who crave evil – from which there is no respite. If Satan controls their life, then Satan has snatched the governance of God's creation and placed it under his control.

Further, if God intended that people should manage His creation, then what can be said of His sovereignty if His creation is now managed by those enslaved to sin? Job clearly understood the implications of our depictions of human nature, and he refused to accept that God has been replaced, or that He was no longer sovereign. Throughout the debate, Job asserts the sovereignty of God, and the defeat of Satan whom he identifies as the monster of the sea, or the gliding serpent. In Job 9, he contends that God created, and continues to control His universe, and "even the monsters of the sea are crushed beneath His feet." Then again in Job 26 he states: "By His skill He crushed the great sea monster, ... and (by) His power pierced the gliding serpent."[36]

4. Regarding God's creation.

We stated with certainty that all people are evildoers. If what was said about all people, was said about one individual, there is no doubt that he/she could sue for slander. For example, if one manager of General Motors were accused of being evil, vile, and corrupt, that person could sue to set the record straight. But who sets the record straight if all their managers are said to be corrupt? Clearly that duty would fall on the corporation because if true, then the entire corporation is corrupt. If not true, then the corporation is clearly slandered.

The same is true of God's creation. We alleged that all God's managers are evil and corrupt. God himself demonstrates this statement to be untrue, when He characterized Job as "a blameless and upright man who shuns evil."[37] To say that all the managers of God's universe are corrupt, is a reflection of God's creation and His governance, and obviously slanders Him. We were considered wise men, and we should have thought through the implications of what we said.

We, of course, knew that God created all people. What we should have asked: is the image of an all powerful, all caring God, enhanced or disparaged by what we said? If it was God's intent that mankind should be the crown of His creation, then what can be said of His power or care if all people are born inherently evil, and remain so for the duration of their lives? What can be said of God's capacity to realize His intent if all people are, because of their inherently corrupt nature, in the service of sin? And what does it say of God the Creator, if the crowns of His creation are no more significant than a maggot or a worm?

Further Considerations

You will recall that in the first part of God's response He directed our attention to his creation. He points to many examples in the inanimate part of His creation to show the enormity of His knowledge, power, creativity, understanding, and governance. He reveals that his creation is wonderfully made. There were no blueprints. The entire universe arose out of His sovereign mind, and His infinite understanding, imagination, wisdom and power. It is vast and full of mystery. It is intricate, delicate and complicated. Much of it is invisible. There are not only the objects that can be seen, but behind these objects are rules that God created under which these objects operate.

The purpose was not to provide a quick lesson on astrology, geology, oceanography or meteorology. Rather it was a lesson in theology. The objective was to comfort Job by validating his perspective, and at the same time correcting us. The God who made this wonderful, intriguing and mysterious universe was also the God who fashioned us. And if He were pleased with His cosmos, (and obviously he was) then why would we assume that the crown of His creation was, already in the womb, evil and corrupt.

I know that we have a sinful nature, but I also know that the Creator of this wonderful world has given me a free will, and the wisdom and understanding to manage His creation accordingly.

Since God called us out for slandering Him, my mind has been opened. I now know that God is not elevated when His creation is denigrated. We were not speaking highly of God, by condemning what He fashioned and made.

Job understood; if what we said was true: i.e., all people are inherently evil, and God punishes those who are evil, then he has no hope. He rightly retorts: "if I say to corruption, 'you are my father,' and to the worm, 'you are my mother or my sister,' where then is my hope? Who can see any hope for me?"[38]

When I read back what we said about humanity, I weep. And when I think of the implications of what we said about humanity's God, I weep even more.

F. The Other Half of the Equation

We now know God was unhappy with us, because we had slandered Him by making disparaging remarks about what He had created. But that was only half of the equation. On the same subject matter, for which God had reprimanded us, He twice praised Job because he had spoken right about Him.[39]

What did Job say that was right?

The point that Job was attempting to make throughout the debate was that he was a man of upright character and blameless conduct. However, we had said that all those born of a woman are inherently evil. If that were true, then what Job said could not be true. Hence, Job immediately took issue with the proposition that all people are born innately evil. His arguments were as follows:

In his initial rebuttal, his first reaction was to point to himself, and say: if I were to die, then I would still have this consolation – that I have not denied the words of the Holy One.[40] Job points to his own righteousness as proof that not all people are born so wicked that it is a certainty that all will sin.

He then addresses God directly in a heart-breaking prayer. My life is coming to an end without hope. Remember, O God that my life is but a breath, and I will never see happiness again. You see me now, but when I die, you will not see me again. You will search for me, but it will be too late. Therefore, I will not keep silent. I will speak out in the anguish of my spirit, I will complain in the bitterness of my soul. If all people are inherently wicked, then why do you have such a high regard for them, and why do you set your heart on them? Surely, it is not to test and punish him.[41]

How have I sinned against you, O you preserver of men? Why have you set me up for punishment by making me bear the burden of a sinful nature that I acquired already in the womb? I cannot change what I was born with, so why don't you simple pardon my transgressions and take away the inherited evil? Because soon I will die, and you will search for me, but I will be no more.[42]

And so his prayer ends. But what does Job mean, when at the beginning, and the end of his prayer he states: "and you will search for me?" Obviously God knows where he is.

Job wants some answers, and he is appealing to God's love, care and the high esteem that He holds for people. Simply put, Job's prayer is: I know that you love me, and value me, and you will search for me to tell what I have done wrong, or if I have sinned, then to pardon me. But do so before it is too late. In other words, Job is attempting to initiate an action from God by reminding Him that He holds people in high regard, that He set his heart on them, and that He cares for them.

In his second response, Job begins by declaring that God's wisdom is profound, and His power is vast.[43] Consequently, if people are inherently wicked, and God punishes the wicked, what hope is there for me? Am I not already found guilty? And if I am already in line for punishment, then why should I struggle in vain? [44]

Moreover, if I am inherently wicked, then even if I washed myself with soap and disinfectant, God would still plunge me into the slime pit of corruption, i.e., I would still be deemed to be corrupt.[45] I would be trapped by a condition over which I had no control, and could do nothing about.

He states that if he had a chance to talk to God, he would say: Don't simply condemn me – tell me what you have against me. What do you gain by oppressing me? Why do you reject me, the work of your own hands?[46] Are you like my friends, in that you search for my faults, and probe after my sin? You know I am not wicked, and yet you are destroying me. I beg of you, remember that you made me, and fashioned me, so why punish me? You guided my conception, and formed me in the womb. You clothed me with skin and flesh, and knit me together with sinews and bones. Throughout my life you have shown me kindness, and in your providence preserved my spirit.[47] Even though I am a righteous man, I cannot lift my head. I am completely confused. If I am being punished because of who I am, then why was I born in the first place?[48]

In his third reply, Job asks us to consider the animals, the birds, and the fish. They also suffer, but they have not sinned. Therefore, how can it be said that suffering is a consequence of wickedness? He states that in God's hand are the souls of every living thing, and the breath of all mankind.[49]

He argues that if we deny his righteousness; then not only are we smearing him with lies, but we are also speaking wickedly and deceitfully, even if we claim to be doing it on God's behalf. If we speak dishonestly, and show partiality, then God will surely rebuke us.[50]

He asserts that notwithstanding our platitudes, he will trust in God; he will continue to do as he had done before, and God will be his deliverance.[51] He challenged us to bring charges of any wrongdoing against him, and if true, he will keep silent.[52] He argues that if mankind is inherently wicked, and there is a certainty that they will sin, then man wastes away like something rotten, like a garment eaten by moths.[53]

On the other hand, God created him and when the period of punishment had passed, God will call him, and he will answer, because God longs for the creature that His hands have made.[54]

In his fourth response, Job reasserts his righteousness. He describes his sufferings and the grief that he is experiencing. He reveals that he put sackcloth on his body, and that his face is foul from weeping, but he assures us that his tribulations are not because of any injustice done by him. He relates that his hands have been free of violence, and is prayer is pure. Furthermore, the witness to his truthfulness is in heaven.[55] In other words, God knows that he is righteous. He then addresses our allegation that human nature is totally corrupt. He declares; if I say to corruption, you are my father, and to the worm, my mother or sister, where then is my hope[56]?

In his fifth rebuttal, Job begins by reminding us that we had always known him to be a man of upright character, and blameless conduct; and yet we had condemned him. He states: you have reproached me many times, and you are not ashamed that what you have said about me is not true.[57] Nonetheless, I know that my Redeemer lives, and I will see Him. How my heart yearns within me, because I know I will be justified. If you are hounding me because you believe that the root of my trouble lies within me, then be afraid, because you are also human, and your sinful nature will also bring His punishment upon you.[58]

In his sixth reply, he addresses our contention that God always punishes the wicked with suffering or poverty. Moreover, because God always punishes the wicked in that way, then suffering or poverty, is itself proof of wickedness.

Job counters by pointing to the inescapable truth that in reality, the wicked often live healthy and prosperous lives. Even those who have no desire to know God's ways, or to pray to Him; escape His punishment.[59] So how can it be said that ill heath or poverty is proof of wickedness? In fact one man dies in full vigor, completely secure, and at ease. Another dies in bitterness of soul, never having enjoyed anything good, but together they lie side by side, and worms cover them both.[60]

I know what you are thinking as you scheme to do me wrong. If I am not wicked, then where is the "great man's" house? But ask those who travel, and they will tell you that evil men do not all suffer, neither are they required to pay for the evil they have done. They go to their grave in peace.[61] If the wicked do not suffer, then how can it be said that my suffering is proof of my wickedness? And if I am not wicked, then how can confession restore me? Do not try to console me with you nonsense. Nothing is left of your answers, but falsehoods.[62]

In his seventh response, Job laments his failure to find God. He suggests that if he were able to speak to Him, he would understand why God was causing him to suffer. He believes that God would not use His power against him. On the contrary, God allows the righteous to dispute with Him, and because he was righteous, his Judge would deliver him forever from his suffering. He believes that his Judge knows how he lived his life, and when He is tried, he will come out as gold. He states: I have always walked in His steps, and obeyed His commands.[63]

He then counters our contention that God always rewards the innocent with health and prosperity. He again points to the inescapable truth that in reality, the innocent often suffer, especially at the hands of the wicked. He observes that the groans of the dying rise from the city, and the souls of the wounded cry out for help. The thrust of his argument is that if the innocent also suffer, then how can it be said that his suffering is the punishment for his sin? He concludes by saying that even though the innocent suffer at the hands of the wicked, God charges no one with wrongdoing. Once again he is making the point that if the wicked are not punished with suffering for their evil deeds, then how can we say that his suffering is proof of wrongdoing? [64]

In his eighth rebuttal, Job is reacting to Bildad's allegation that his dreadful punishment is akin to the punishment suffered by the wicked, and is therefore, proof of his wickedness.[65]

Job responds by declaring: God forbid that I should ever justify what you have said. As long as I live, I will tell the truth. I will not speak wickedly or deceitfully. I will not deny my integrity. I will maintain my righteousness, and never let it go. My conscience will not reproach me for as long as I live.[66]

In his ninth and final reply, Job gives the most extensive defense of his upright character and blameless conduct. He begins by conveying God's will for all people. It is to revere God and shun evil.[67]

We had argued that God's will for Job was to fear the punishment of God, and to confess to those inherited sins that he had acquired because he was born of a woman, and also to those overt sins that would inevitably arise from his sinful nature. In other word, we were asking him to confess to a wicked condition that he was unable to change, and to sins that that he was unable to avoid.

Job counters by describing how he was honored and respected because: I put on righteousness as my clothing and justice as my robe, and also; because I was always mindful that He who made me in the womb also made my servants.[68]

He wonders; what has God above chosen for us? What is our inheritance from the Almighty? Is it calamity for the wicked and misfortune for those who do evil – which is what we had argued? Is that what He is watching for?[69] He argues that even by those standards, he would be vindicated. He wants God to weigh him on the scales of justice, because God knows that he is a man of integrity. He then recites the details of his life and concludes: my desire is that the Almighty would answer me, and that my adversaries write out the charges against me. I would face the accusations proudly; I would wear it as a crown. I would tell Him exactly what I had done; I would come before Him as a prince.[70]

Observations

As previously noted, Zophar, Bildad and I, perceived people as corrupt, and they remained so for the duration of their lives. Consequently, we believed that when God interacted with people, He did so chiefly as a Judge, fully capable and willing to punish the perpetual delinquents, and to restore the health and wealth of those who confessed their misdeeds.

Job's perception of God was not primarily as a Judge of people, but as their Creator. As a result, he believed that God interacts with people, not firstly as the Judge of delinquents, but as the Creator of His children. He relates that God made all people, that He guided their conception, and formed them in the womb. He then clothed them with skin and flesh, and knitted them together with sinews and bones. Moreover, as their Creator, He highly values what His hands had made, he sets His heart on them, He shows them kindness, and in His providence He preserves their spirit.

In part one of His response, God validates Job's perception of Him. He does so by taking Job on a cosmic tour, and He identified himself as the Creator of everything that Job saw. Not once does He refer to himself as a Judge.

When God concluded His address, Job was indeed vindicated. God twice comforted him by confirming the validity of what he said. He also twice reprimanded us for our folly. By saying it twice, God was leaving no doubt as to who spoke right about Him.

G. Self-assessment

I have summarized the debate, and experienced God's negative reaction to what we said. It is now time to face defeat, and evaluate what we said in light of what we knew at the time. The question is: apart from Job's arguments, and the reasons for God's admonishment, should we have known better? Or to put it another way: if neither Job nor God had said anything, were there reasons to believe that we were wrong?

Specifically I wish to examine two of the statements that God found offensive. They are: all people are born, totally evil, vile and corrupt, and; all people are involuntarily enslaved to their sinful nature for the duration of their lives. For this assessment, I will speak only for myself.

1. I had always had the greatest admiration for Job. If, before the debate someone had asked me to describe him, I would have said; he was upright in character and blameless in conduct. And yet, it was I who led the charge against him by impugning his character, and accusing him of various disgraceful sins. The entire onslaught was based solely on a religious belief. Job accused me of betraying him, and I did. The depth of my regret and remorse knows no limit. Job forgave me, but the spectacle of what I did haunted me till I died.
2. The statements fly in the face of reality. As it turned out, Bildad and Zophar were wrong in their theology, but they were not totally evil, vile, and corrupt. I had always known them to be good, fair, loyal and generous. So too,

were many others: in my family, among my neighbors, and among my other friends. What shames me now, is that I knew it even then. Job had told us to be careful in what we said, because we were also human, and he was right.
3. The statements were even contrary to my experience of myself. I generally tried to live an exemplary life, and to the extent that I was successful, I was not totally evil.
4. I now realize that my contention that all people are born evil, vile and corrupt, that they drink up evil like water, and that they remain so for their entire life; was wrong. I had painted everyone with the same brush. I now acknowledge, what every high school teacher has always known, i.e., some people have a better character than others.
5. If all people drink up sin like water, because they crave it, and are unable to save themselves from their cravings, then their will is enslaved. I now believe that the statement is a religious delusion. Throughout my entire life I experienced a "free will." Every day I made choices between good and bad, and I saw others do the same. The idea that I could only "will" to do evil, or that I could not "will" to do good, seems alien to me now.
6. The statements strip people of their responsibility. People are only responsible for their actions if they have a choice. If they are involuntarily enslaved to sin already at birth, and remain so for the duration of their lives, then they are robots, and not responsible for whom they are, and what they do.
7. More important however, I could have, and should have known that the statements are disparaging of God and His creation. I of course knew that God was the Creator of all things, including all of mankind. To say of these people, that they are born totally corrupt, is an insult to the God who created them.

H. Conclusion

Needless to say, Job and I had, on many occasions spoken of God's reaction. After all, it was by far the most significant factor in the lives of all four of us. The last conversation was on my deathbed, and my dear friend Job, was present.

At the time of my death, he was once again considered the greatest man in the East. His health and prosperity had been restored. He was twice as wealthy as before. He had a new family consisting of seven sons and three daughters. His sons respected him, and his daughters adored him. He was active in the community, and was honored and respected by everyone.

The irony of our changing's circumstances did not escape me. At the time of our debate, Job was diseased, frail, and repulsive, and yet he argued that God had created him, and therefore had a high regard for him; that He magnified him, that He paid close attention to him, and that He longed for the person that His hands had made. At the same time, my other two friends and I were strong, healthy, and well fed, arguing that he was, already at birth, evil and corrupt. In the eyes of God he was no more significant then a maggot or a worm.

Now I was sick, frail, emaciated and dying. I was looking to Job for comfort, friendship and support – something that I had failed to give to him. I felt it was time to apologize again, and to give my friend a poem I had written for him.

To Job – My Dear Friend and Mentor

My dear friend Job, had it all:
Health and wealth, and servants at call,
A beautiful wife, and ten children to share,
His love, and wealth, and bountiful care.

A New Perspective on the Book of Job

He helped the lame, the poor, and the blind,
He was generous, helpful, understanding and kind.
He was a good man: honest and fair,
Treating his servants with kindness and care.

Then one day the good life ended,
And Job's life was left suspended.
His wealth had vanished; his children were dead,
He had very little left, except for a bed.

When we came to see him, we were shocked,
And for seven long days, no one talked.
He was wrapped in scabs, and contorted by pain:
He wanted to die; he had nothing to gain.

The question was: why was he suffering and sad?
We told him it was: because you are bad.
You were born of a woman, and therefore corrupt.
You are evil and vile, and morally bankrupt.

You are a flesh-eating maggot; a useless worm,
No more important than a tiny germ.
But you can be restored, if you swallow your pride,
And acknowledged your sins, and return to God's side.

But Job said: God made me from clay,
And preserved my spirit from day to day.
He clothed my body with flesh and skin,
And formed the organs found within.

He fashioned me with care and skill,
And gifted me with an active will.
So how can I be evil when God made me good?
What you have said is a blatant falsehood.

Why would God spurn the man He had made?
Was life no more than a cruel charade?
Am I to be punished with no way out,
For something I can do nothing about?

And so it continued till God set us straight,
Job had been right throughout the debate.
People are the crown of God's creation,
But we had made them an aberration.

We had denigrated His work, and said it was vile,
What God had made was not worthwhile.
And God was angry, and he told us twice,
To repent of our slander, and to sacrifice.

I have thought and thought for countless times,
About my words, and moral crimes.
My heart was ungrateful, devoid of a song,
The import of my words was entirely wrong.

I earnestly pray with all my heart,
That God will forgive me for my part.
Because He holds in His hands my DNA,
And fashioned me from dust and clay.

From conception, through gestation,
He forms the crowns of His creation.
So I need not be afraid,
He will not spurn what He has made.

Therefore dear Job, it is time for me,
To leave you with an apology.
I was wrong, and you were right:
We are precious in God's sight.

With love and gratitude,
Eliphaz

"Tell me again why God approved of what you said," I whispered.

Job took my hand. "No, my dear Eliphaz," he answered tenderly. "I will tell you why He approves of you. It all begins by taking God at His word when He told us that He is the Creator of this universe. Because He is perfect, He can only create what is good. So when He created you, my long and cherished friend, you too were good. He gave you a free will, and despite some bad choices that you may have made, He loved you. Throughout your life He cared for you, and demonstrated His thoughtfulness for you. And know this: God does not reject the work of His hands. On the contrary, He longs for you, and He is now calling for you."

With that he hugged me, and I slipped into the overwhelming and all-embracing love of Him who made me.

CHAPTER 8

POST SCRIPT

As previously noted, when I moved to the afterlife, I was given the gift of timelessness. As a result, I am able to move backward and forward in time, and to see events, and to read publications and commentaries on our debate that arose subsequent to my death. In this chapter I wish to comment on two ensuing matters: the introduction of Elihu, and theories as to why God was angry with us.

The Appearance of Elihu

Whoever interjected Elihu into the debate did so by alleging that he became very angry with Job for justifying himself rather than God. He was also angry with us, because we had not found a way to refute Job, and yet had condemned him. He had waited before speaking because we were older than him. But when he saw that we had nothing more to say, he decided to speak.[1]

The fact is there was no such person. His speeches were added long after my death. Many scholars have concluded the same.

The writers of *The New Bible Commentary* had this to say about Elihu: "most scholars think that the four speeches of Elihu are a later addition to the book of Job. It is strange that Elihu is not mentioned in the prologue, ... but it is even stranger that he is not mentioned in the epilogue, although the other friends are. Furthermore, the Elihu speeches also delay God's reply to Job, which we might have expected immediately after ch. 31, where 'the words of Job are ended' (31:40). When God does reply (chs. 38-40) he speaks as if nothing has intervened. So it is often thought that Elihu is the creation of a later pious author who was unhappy with the failure of Job's friends to answer his arguments and unhappy also with the way the divine speeches come to no definite conclusion."[2]

If the pious author's motivation for interjecting Elihu into the debate was because "the divine speeches came to no definite conclusion" he was wrong. As we have seen, the "divine speeches" came to a very definite conclusion, mostly at our expense. It should also be noted that when God reprimanded us, He at the same time approved of what Job had said. Specifically God said that we had not spoken the truth about Him "as my servant Job had." Consequently, when Elihu supposedly became angry with Job for justifying himself rather than God, he was as wrong as we were. He would therefore have been included in God's rebuke, had he existed.

Richard R. Losch, a retired Episcopal Priest, now author, and a former Rector of the St. James Episcopal Church, also contends that Elihu was a Johnny-come-lately. In his book: *All the People in the Bible* he writes: "The dialogue with Elihu is believed to have been a later addition to the Book of Job. While the dialogue with the other three is on a basic level of practical theology that might have been expected in the earlier days of the Jewish faith, that with Elihu takes the discussion to a much more elevated level of theology that is more akin to the thinking of the early rabbinical period. Elihu sees God as transcendent and above human comprehension, to be worshipped and obeyed, but not understood."[3]

In their introduction to the Book of Job, the writers of *The New Oxford Annotated Bible* categorically conclude: "A later poet contributed Elihu's speeches."[4] Later they explain why they arrived at such a conclusion: "Most commentaries believe that these chapters (32 – 37) with their peculiar language (containing many Aramaic words) and different style (the new speaker seems to quote ... the yet-undelivered discourse of the Lord), belong to a later hand than that of the poet."[5]

The writers for *Wikipedia* have this to say about the discourses of Elihu. "Some question the status of Elihu's interruption and the didactic sermon because of his sudden appearance and disappearance from the text. Even scholars who regard the Book of Job as a literary composition by a single author tend to see Elihu's speeches as an early addition or commentary to the original book. He is not mentioned in Job 2:11, in which Job's friends were introduced, nor is he mentioned at all in the epilogue, 42:7-10, in which God expresses anger at Job's friends. He does not say anything that is not said more succinctly by the original friends or by God, and his speech contains more Aramaisms than the rest of the book."[6]

For the reasons stated above, he will not be referred to hereafter.

Theories as to why God was angry

I note with some surprise that there is no consensus among the various commentaries as to why God was angry with us. Some theories of why they believe He was angry are as follows.[7]

1. *The Pulpit Bible Commentary* restates the question but doesn't even attempt an explanation. It states; "Job had, on the whole, spoken what was right and true of God.... The 'comforters,' consciously or unconsciously, had spoken what was false. Even if they had said what they believed, they ought to have known better."

2. *Ellicott's Commentary for English Readers* had this to say: "The verdict that is spoken against the friends of Job is based rather on the tone and spirit of what they said than on any of their actual words, for many of these are conspicuous for their wisdom, truth and beauty. But throughout they had been on the wrong side, and seemed to think that the cause of God had need to be upheld at all risks, and that it might even be required to tell lies for God (Job 13:7); and it was that that provoked the Divine indignation."

3. Others such as *Barnes Notes* provide a hypothesis, but no explanation to support it. It theorizes that although God was angry with everyone, He was less angry with Job because "his arguments tended to vindicate the divine character and to uphold the divine government."
4. *Wesley's Notes* also suggest that God's anger is not to be understood absolutely, but comparatively. "Job was not so much to be blamed as his friends because his opinion concerning the methods of God's providence, and God's attitude towards good and bad men was truer than theirs."
5. *The Jamieson-Fausset-Brown Bible Commentary* asserts that God was angry with the friends because: "their spirit towards Job was unkindly, and to justify themselves in their unkindness they used false arguments (namely, that calamities always prove peculiar quilt); therefore, though it was 'for God'; they spoke thus falsely (and) God 'reproves' them."
6. In a convoluted argument, *Clarke's Commentary* suggests that if we are to understand why God was angry, we must consider what was said in light of the next life. "It will be difficult to find anything in the speeches of Eliphaz and his companions which should make the difference here supposed, if we set aside the doctrine of a future state; for in this view the others would speak more worthily of God than Job, by endeavoring to vindicate his providence in the exact distribution of good and evil in this life: whereas Job's assertion, in Job 9:22, that ... 'He destroys the perfect and the wicked,' ... would, upon this supposition be directly charging God that He made no distinction between the good and the bad. But now, take the other life into account, and the thing will appear in quite a contrary light; and we shall easily see the reason why

God approves the sentiments of Job, and condemns those of the friends."
7. John Gill, in his commentary, *Gill's Exposition of the Entire Bible* states that one of the reasons that God was angry with us was, "for charging Job falsely, and condemning him; which provoked the Lord, and caused His wrath to be kindled like fire."
8. The writers of *The New Bible Commentary* posit another explanation. "How can the friends' respectful talk about God be called folly? It can only be that the friends spoke of God entirely in the third person, as an object, whereas Job insisted on addressing God personally."[8]

Unfortunately, none of the differing explanations are accurate. I believe that the reason that scholars were unable to agree on the cause of God's anger was because they failed to identify our offending statements.

There are two theories however, that deserve additional consideration.

First, my friends and I said that God punished Job with suffering, when in fact He did not. We now know that it was Satan who brought on Job's tribulations. Nonetheless, this assertion was not the one that angered God. The defamatory statement had to be something different from what Job had said, and in this case Job thought and said the same thing.[9]

There was however, another matter over which we sharply disagreed. We said that God always punishes the wicked with suffering and/or poverty, and always causes the innocent to prosper, when in fact He does not. The question is: was this the statement that caused God to become angry with us?

There are those who believe it was. In his commentary Matthew Henry writes: "Job's friends had wronged God by making prosperity a mark of the true church, and affliction a certain proof of God's wrath."[10]

Benson agrees. He states that God was angry "because they (referring to my friends and me) had laid it down as a certain maxim, that all, without exception, who were afflicted with such grievous calamities as Job was, must needs be under the wrath of God, as being guilty of some notorious crime: and that all who passed through life in prosperity must needs be accounted as righteous in the eyes of God."[11]

Although our statements were altogether false, for the reasons that follow, it was not the cause of God's anger toward us.

1. To say that God always rewards the innocent and always punishes the wicked was the accepted orthodox theology of our day.[12] The following passages demonstrate how in the Old Testament, God himself describes His rewards and punishments in almost the same words as that used by my friends and me.

a) <u>I will begin with the proposition that God always causes the innocent to prosper.</u>

In Leviticus 26, God states: "If you follow my decrees and are careful to obey my commands, I will send you rain in its season, and the ground will yield its crops, and the trees of the field their fruit…. You will eat all the food you want and live in safety in your land…. I will look on you with favor and make you fruitful and increase your numbers…."[13]

In Deuteronomy 28, God repeats this promise. "If you keep the commands of the Lord your God and walk in His ways … the Lord will grant you abundant prosperity…. If you pay attention to the commands of the Lord your God … you will always be at the top, never at the bottom."[14]

b) <u>Turning now to the proposition that God always punishes the wicked.</u>

In Leviticus 26, we read: "but if you do not listen to me and carry out all these commands … then I will do this to you: I will bring upon you sudden terror, wasting diseases and fever that will destroy your sight and drain away your life…." God then emphasizes the certainty of these punishments if His people are disobedient. Four times He states: "If after this you will not listen to me, I will punish you for your sins seven times over."[15] In the Bible the number 7 denotes certainty, completeness or fullness. So when God promises to punish the disobedient "seven times over", He is making it clear that He will do as He promises.

God's punishments are revisited in Deuteronomy 28. "If you do not obey the Lord your God and do not carefully follow all His commands and decrees, the Lord will plague you with diseases until he has destroyed you.... The Lord will strike you with wasting disease, with fever and inflammation.... The Lord will afflict you with boils ... and with tumors, festering sores and the itch, from which you cannot be cured ... spreading from the soles of your feet to the top of your head.... All these curses will come upon you. They will pursue you and overtake you until you are destroyed.... They will be a sign and a wonder to you and your descendants forever.... Just as it pleased the Lord to make you prosper and increase in number, so it will please him to ruin and destroy you."[16] Deuteronomy 28:33, is translated in the KJV to say; if the people do not obey, they will be "oppressed and crushed always."

Given God's express words, can we be faulted for believing what we did?

Even the prophets thought that God would always punish the wicked. Isaiah predicts: "The day of the Lord is coming—a cruel day, with wrath and fierce anger.... I will punish the world for its evil, the wicked for their sins."[17] Later he declares the certainty of God doing what He plans or purposes to do. "The Lord Almighty has sworn, 'Surely, as I have planned, so it will be, and as I have purposed, so it will stand.'"[18] Jeremiah is equally direct. He writes: "This will be the sign to you that I will punish you in this place, declares the Lord, so that you may know that my threats of harm against you will surely stand."[19] In Numbers, God instructs Balaam to ask Balak the following rhetorical question: "Does He (God) speak and then not act? Does He promise and not fulfill?"[20] The message of Zephaniah is similar. "At that time I will search Jerusalem with lamps and punish those who are complacent ... who think that the Lord will do nothing."[21]

We now know that God does not always reward the obedient or punish the disobedient. However, it is not likely that God would be angry with us for an opinion that was shared by Moses, and at least some of the prophets.

2. There is another reason why our statements, that God always rewards the obedient and punishes the disobedient, did not offend God. As we have seen the offensive statements must also be disparaging of God in some way. Throughout the Old Testament, God regularly caused the wicked to suffer and the innocent to prosper. Moses had explicitly said: "just as it pleased the Lord to make you prosper and increase in number, so it will please Him to ruin and destroy you."[22]

Job's position was: "God destroys both the blameless and the wicked. When a scourge brings sudden death he mocks the despair of the innocent. When a land falls into the hands of the wicked, he blindfolds its judges ... while He smiles on the schemes of the wicked. ... Those who provoke God are secure."[23] Surely God's character or reputation is not enhanced by the suggestion that He mocks the despair of the innocent and smiles on the schemes of the wicked.

In chapter 14, Job complains that: "as water wears away stones, and torrents wash away the soil, so you destroy man's hope."[24] In the meantime the wicked live on, growing old, and increasing in power? "They see their children established around them, their offspring before their eyes. Their homes are safe and free from fear; the rod of God is not upon them.... They spend their years in prosperity and go down to the grave in peace."[25] Obviously Job is accusing God of treating him (a righteous man) more severely than the wicked. How are Job's statements less disparaging of God than our statements?

3. God had accused my friends and me, of not speaking of Him, "what is right, as my servant Job has"? The question then is: Was Job right when he said that God also causes the innocent to suffer? The answer is no. God made it quite clear that He causes no one to suffer. Suffering is simply a part of nature. Our statements that God always causes the innocent to prosper and the wicked to suffer were no more wrong then Job's statement. Both were wrong, albeit for different reasons. Consequently, our statements could not have been the statements that so offended God.

4. The statement that God always rewards the righteous and always punishes the wicked, was not the essence of the debate. The debate initially arose when Job accused God of causing him (a righteous man) to suffer. The point of all our arguments was to convince Job that he was not a righteous man. This was just one statement in one argument, used to refute his claim to righteousness. Our main argument was that he could not be a righteous man, because his nature, like everyone else born of a woman, was corrupt.

PART TWO

THE BOOK OF JOB APPLIED

CHAPTER 9

THE CHANGING CONCEPT OF HUMAN NATURE

A. Introduction

Throughout our dispute with Job, we had experienced a number of surprises – none greater then when God accused us of slander. But there was still one surprise to come that occurred thousands of years after I was laid to rest. Once again I rely on my capacity to transcend time, and to comment on all events and publications that have arisen since my death.

In 1618-19 a document surfaced that my friends and I could very well have written. The document came to known as: *The Canons of Dort*, which was an elaboration of a previous document called, *The Confession of Faith*. In part, both of these documents teach what we preached, and which earned us God's reprimand. And yet, both are Standards in many Calvinistic Churches. These Standards are interpretations of Scripture that the various denominations have accepted as correct. Some churches such as the Christian Reformed Church, compel all their office bearers, including pastors, elders, deacons and seminary professors, to defend and promote them.

Before I analyze these documents, it may be beneficial to learn how both of these documents came into existence, and for that we must go back to St. Augustine.

B. Historical Review

1. St. Augustine (354-430)

His Life.
Augustine was born in Tagaste, a city in Northern Africa. His mother, Monica, was a devout Christian, but his philandering father was not. Although Augustine is now referred to as a saint, that would certainly not be descriptive of his early life. As a young man, Augustine followed in the footsteps of his father, and pursued an active hedonistic lifestyle. In his candid autobiography, *Confessions*, he portrays his youthful life as one addicted to pleasure.

He eventually moved to Milan, Italy, where he taught rhetoric. While there, he was profoundly influenced by the writings and sermons of St. Ambrose, the bishop of Milan. In 386 he decided to accept the Christian faith, and was baptized by St. Ambrose the following year. Shortly thereafter he returned to North Africa, and in 391, he was ordained a priest. He was then appointed to serve a church in Hippo, a town near the city in which he was born. He served in that capacity until he died in 430.

During his priesthood he wrote zealously, creating several books, including his autobiography. However, most of his writings consisted of correspondence to friends, enemies, perceived heretics, other priests, various bishops and churches. As he grew older, his theology morphed, from what was then known as orthodox Christianity, into what can now be described as Calvinism.

In her well researched book: *Adam, Eve and the Serpent*, Professor Elaine Pagels examines the teachings of the early church, from the death of Christ until the death of St. Augustine, more than 400 years later.[1]

She relates that in his early ministry, Augustine was in line with all the great leaders of the early church. He earnestly taught that all people were created in the image of God, and as a result had an exulted position, capable of choosing between good and evil. However, as he grew older his theology changed, and toward the end of his ministry, he denied the goodness of God's creation, and the freedom of the will.

In so doing, he came into conflict with almost all of the leaders in the orthodox community, one of which was Pelagius, a devout scholar and philosopher from Britain. Professor Pagels describes the conflict as follows. "By 417, the city of Rome was so divided between the supporters and opponents of Pelagius that partisans of both sides had actually rioted in the streets. Two years earlier, two councils of bishops in Palestine had declared Pelagius orthodox; but two opposing councils of African bishops, led by Augustine and his colleagues, condemned him, and persuaded Pope Innocent, bishop of Rome, to take their side. When Innocent died, his successor, Pope Zosimus, at first declared Pelagius's teachings orthodox; but after receiving vehement protests from Augustine and other African bishops, he reversed himself, and excommunicated Pelagius.

During the battle against Pelagius and his advocates, many of them influential Romans, Augustine and his colleagues openly courted the emperor's support. Augustine's friend and fellow African bishop Alypius, brought eighty Numidian stallions as bribes to the imperial court, and successfully lobbied there against Pelagius. The result gratified Augustine: in April 418, not only did the pope excommunicate Pelagius, but the emperor Honorius condemned the newly declared heretic, and ordered him fined, expelled from office, and exiled."[2]

His Teachings

According to Professor Pagels, it was Augustine who, "effectively transformed much of the teaching of the Christian faith. Instead of the freedom of the will and humanity's original royal dignity, Augustine emphasizes humanity's enslavement to sin."[3] It was St. Augustine who introduced the concept "that infants are infected from the moment of conception with the disease of original sin...."[4] Professor Pagels notes that the concept of original sin, i.e., all people are born totally corrupt, was a concept, not accepted, or taught by the early church.

But how was Adam's original sin transmitted to his descendents? In his book, *The City of God*[5], Augustine writes: "(Adam) being willingly depraved and justly condemned, begot all his offspring under the same depravation and condemnation: for in him were we all, when he ... corrupted us all.... We had not our particular forms yet, but there was the seed of our natural propagation, which being corrupted by sin must needs produce man of that same nature, the slave to sin, and the object of just condemnation."

What this means, according to Professor Pagels is, "that the semen itself already 'shackled by the bond of death,' transmits the damage incurred by sin. Hence ... every human being ever conceived through semen already is born contaminated with sin."[6] This also explains why Christ was sinless.

About one thousand years later, the concept of original sin was accepted by John Calvin, taught to Guido de Bres, and fully developed by the Synod of Dort.

2. John Calvin (1509 – 1564)

His Life[7]

Calvin was born in Noyon, France, and educated in Paris as a lawyer. His father was a lawyer for the Catholic Church. After his father's death in 1531, Calvin studied Greek and Latin at the University of Paris.

Calvin had a number of theological differences with the Catholic Church, so in 1533, he declared himself a Protestant. The timing could not have been worse. France was predominately Catholic, and widespread violence erupted against the Protestants. Consequently, Calvin, his brother, his sister and two friends, fled to Basel, Switzerland, where in 1536, he published: *The Institutes of the Christian Religion*. In his book, he accepts and develops the teachings of St. Augustine, in respect to human nature and original sin.

In the same year he accepted an invitation from William Farel to assist him as a co-pastor of a church in Geneva, Switzerland, that Farel had founded. Calvin preached regularly, but unfortunately his message was not well received, and the governing council expelled both men.

Following his expulsion, Calvin moved to Strasbourg, Germany, where he became the lead pastor of another church. In the meantime, the church in Geneva realized that they lacked political and spiritual leadership, and in 1541 invited him back. Calvin accepted, and from then until his death in 1564, he was the pastor of his former church.

The low point of Calvin's life came as a result of his involvement with Michael Servetus, a renegade, and notorious theologian. In about 1546, Calvin and Servetus were brought together by a mutual acquaintance. Thereafter, through a series of writings, including a large number of letters addressed to Calvin, Servetus strongly criticized Calvin's doctrine of predestination. What made Calvin particularly angry was that Servetus sent him a copy of his own Institutes, liberally annotated with counter arguments. After receiving these "corrections", and upon learning that Servetus planned to pass through Geneva, Calvin wrote a letter to a friend stating that if Servetus were to come; "then as far as my authority goes, I would not let him leave alive."

In 1553, Servetus, on his way to Italy, did stop in Geneva where he was recognized and arrested. Calvin had his secretary write a letter, addressed to the court, accusing Servetus of heresy. According to the Encyclopedia Britannia, Calvin played a prominent part in his trial, and pressed for execution. After a lengthy trial he was found guilty, and five days after his sentencing, on October 27, 1553, he was burned alive.

His Teachings

Calvin begins his Institutes under the heading: "Through The Fall and Revolt of Adam, The whole Human Race made Accursed and Degenerate of Original Sin." What follows are a number of quotes taken from this section.[8]

"All of us, therefore, descending from an impure seed, come into the world tainted with the contagion of sin. Nay, before we behold the light of the sun we are in God's sight defiled and polluted." (Par. 5)

"We thus see that the impurity of parents is transmitted to their children, so that all, without exception, are originally depraved." (Par. 6)

"It should be enough for us to know that Adam was made the depository of the endowments which God was pleased to bestow on human nature, and that, therefore, when he lost what he had received, he lost not only for himself but for us all.... There is nothing absurd, therefore, in the view, that when he was divested, his nature was left naked and destitute, that he having been defiled by sin, the pollution extends to all his seed. Thus, from a corrupt root, corrupt branches proceeding; transmit their corruption to the saplings, which spring from them. The children being vitiated in their parent, conveyed the taint to the grandchildren; in other words, corruption commencing in Adam, is, by perpetual descent, conveyed from those proceeding to those coming after them." (Par. 7)

"Hence, even infants bringing their condemnation with them from their mother's womb, suffer not for another's, but for their own defect. For although they have not yet produced the fruits of their own unrighteousness, they have the seed implanted in them. Nay, their whole nature is, as it were, a seed-bed of sin, and therefore cannot but be odious and abominable to God." (Par. 8)

3. Guido de Bres (1522-1567)

His Life[9]

De Bres was born in 1522, in Mons, a city located in an area then called the low country. Today this area incorporates the whole of Belgium and the Netherlands. Five years before his birth, Martin Luther had created a theological and political firestorm when he nailed his ninety-five theses to the door of a Catholic church in Wittenberg. It was into this ongoing firestorm that Guido grew up. In 1547, at the age of 25, he joined the reformers – all of whom were deemed to be heretics by Phillip II, the King of Spain. He controlled much of Europe at that time, and under his rule, all heretics were subject to severe punishment.

In 1548, de Bres traveled to England, which at that time, provided a safe haven for Protestants, and especially those involved in the reform movement. While in England he studied theology.

In 1552, he returned to the low country, and at great risk to himself, became an itinerant preacher. To mitigate the risk, he traveled under a false name, and the church services were held in secret. Passwords were necessary.

In 1556, Phillip II began to severely persecute all non-Catholics, driving the reform movement even further underground. It was during this period that de Bres met John Calvin. The meeting must have made a positive impression, because in 1558, he went to Geneva to study under Calvin.

In 1559, he returned to the low lands, and continued his secret ministry. Because his ministry was essentially made up of small groups meeting in different houses, various "leaders" would take over in his absence. Some of these leaders would develop their own homespun theology.

At that time there was a great deal of dissatisfaction in the Catholic Church. Much of the unhappiness and resentment arose from various corrupt practices including bribes, patronage appointments, and the sale of God's forgiveness. These sales were called indulgences.

From a theological point of view however, Pastor de Bres' greatest challenge was neither the homespun theologies, nor the Catholic Church. Ever since the death of Christ a number of sects, movements, and other religious groups had emerged, which he considered heretical. These groups were also competing for the affections of the populace.

Pastor de Bres did not want his small flocks to be distracted by these so-called sects. Therefore, to keep his followers on message, and because the written word was considered more authoritative than the spoken word, he began to write his *Confession of Faith*, (Confession) which he completed in 1561. It is often referred to as the Belgic Confession, because it was written in a region now known as Belgium. In his Confession he identifies by name, at least twelve sects or groups that he believed were heretical.

As long as his ministry remained small and secret, his followers met only mild opposition. The local Catholic authorities had little appetite for confrontation, especially those involving intra-sectarian squabbles. However, that all changed in 1561. One evening, under the leadership of one of Pastor de Bres' students, a large group of Protestants marched through the main street of Doornik, a city in the low country, singing hymns. The local bishop immediately launched an investigation, and soon all fingers were pointing at de Bres; but he had gone into hiding, and could not be found.

Eventually he agreed to a plan whereby the reformers would present Phillip II with a copy of his Confession. It was hoped that upon reading the Confession, Phillip would agree that the reformers were not the enemy. Specifically, the reformers were relying on Article XXXVI that provides:

1. Governments are appointed by God to punish evildoers and protect those that do well.
2. It is the duty of every citizen to subject himself to the magistrates: to pay tribute, to show due honor and respect to them, and to obey them in all things which are not repugnant to the word of God.
3. Wherefore we detest the Anabaptists and other seditious people, and in general all those who reject the higher powers and magistrates....

It was particularly the third provision upon which the reformers relied. The Anabaptists openly promoted the rejection of all government authority, and it was hoped that Phillip would see the reformers as an ally against a common enemy.

Pursuant to the plan, someone threw a copy of the Confession, along with a letter addressed to Phillip II, over the castle wall of a local Catholic authority. As anticipated, the Confession found its way to the King, but it had the opposite effect hoped for. The search for de Bres intensified, but he and his family escaped to an area near the French border. There he continued to minister for a number of years. His ministry flourished and by 1566 he was preaching to large crowds. When Phillip heard of these crowds, he sent troops to quell what he perceived to be an insurrection. Eventually de Bres was captured, and on May 31, 1567 he was hanged.

His Teachings[10]

In respect to original sin, Pastor de Bres taught: "As a result of Adam's sin, man corrupted his whole nature ... (and thus became) wicked, perverse and corrupt in all his ways.... Man is but a slave to sin.... We believe that through the disobedience of Adam, original sin is extended to all mankind; which is a corruption of the whole nature and a hereditary disease, wherewith even infants in their mother's womb are infected, and which produces in man all sorts of sin, being in him as a root thereof, and therefore is so vile and abominable in the sight of God that it is sufficient to condemn all mankind."

4. The formation of the Canons of Dort[11]

Jacob Arminius (1560-1609) was a professor of theology at the University of Leyden in the Netherlands. He did not accept a number of doctrines as set out in Pastor de Bres' Confession. One year after the death of Arminius, his followers, (called the Remonstrants) circulated a position paper articulating their differences with the Confession. The position paper contained five articles. Each article explained the Remonstrants' perspective in respect to five contentious doctrines, including the doctrine of original sin.

It didn't take long and people began to take sides. The Calvinists sided with Pastor de Bres, and almost all the other denominational groups, including the Lutherans, sided with the Remonstrants.

What further complicated matters was that during this period the Dutch were in the middle of an eighty-year war for independence from Spain (1568 – 1649). In 1609 a truce was called which lasted until 1621, after which war resumed. Many of the Dutch military and political leaders were Calvinists.

In his writings, Calvin departed from the orthodox position that, "the powers that be are ordained by God." He defended the right of people to fight against oppressive governments, that the Dutch perceived Spain to be. Encouraged by Calvin's writings, the Calvinists were fiercely patriotic. Inevitably, patriotism and theology began to mix.

The Remonstrants also opposed the Spanish occupation. But they were less vociferous because they continued to believe that civil authorities were ordained by God, and had the right to interfere in religious disputes for the purpose of promoting peace. As a result they were perceived to be sympathetic to Spain. In fact, during this time some Remonstrant leaders were arrested for treason. The conflict between the two groups became so hateful and divisive, that it almost led to a civil war.

Therefore, in 1618-1619, at the request of the Remonstrants, and at the urging of the Dutch government, the Reformed Churches of the Netherlands held a Synod in the Dutch Reformed Church, in the city of Dordrecht. There were 99 voting delegates – all men. The Synod (now called the Synod of Dort) held 154 sessions over a period of seven months. Initially thirteen Remonstrants were seated.

A major point of contention was the status attributed to the Remonstrants. They were the first to ask for the Synod, and they expected to be treated as equals: both in terms of the number of delegates, as well as their participation in the Synod. Instead they were assigned 13 out of 99 seats. In respect to their participation, they were treated like defendants, and they complained constantly. In protest, they often argued at length over procedural matters. Consequently, under the leadership of the moderator, Johannes Bogerman, the thirteen Remonstrants were all dismissed. Some delegates were upset by Bogerman's conduct, but no steps were taken to rectify the wrong. All of the remaining delegates were from the Calvinist side, and hence were predisposed in favor of the Confession.

Ostensibly, the question to be considered was whether the views contained in the Remonstrants' position paper could be reconciled with the Confession. It is clear however, that the question was only a pretence to fairness. Everyone knew there could be no reconciliation. The absence of reconciliation was the reason the Synod was convened in the first place. The real purpose was to refute the Remonstrants.

Once the thirteen Remonstrants were dismissed, and because there was no one left to speak for them, the Synod moved quickly. Each article in the position paper was condemned in writing, in what came to be known as *The*

Canons of Dort, (Canons). Not surprising, the remaining 86 delegates all voted in favor of the Canons. They had accomplished their purpose. It was this Synod that fully formulated the doctrine of the total depravity of human nature.

C. Human nature as taught by the Canons

The Synod of Dort classifies reality into two categories, namely: matters relating to the spiritual aspect of human nature, and maters relating to things natural and civil.

1. Regarding the Spiritual aspect:
The Canons teach that everyone is spiritually dead unless they have been regenerated. What it means to be spiritually dead is described in Chapters III and IV, Articles 1-3, and 16.

Article 1
After the fall:
1. All people became involved in blindness of mind, horrible darkness, vanity, and perverseness of judgment.
2. All people became wicked, rebellious, and obdurate in heart and will, and impure in their affections.

Article 2
After the fall, all the posterity of Adam …
1. Derived corruption from their original parent, and
2. Gave birth to children in their own likeness. Therefore:
    a. All their children are corrupt by nature and
    b. Deserving of the just judgment of God.

Article 3
1. After the fall, all people are:
    a. Conceived in sin.
    b. Children of wrath.

c. Incapable of saving good.
d. Prone to evil.
e. Dead in sin, and in bondage thereto.
2. Further, because people are without the regenerating grace of the Holy Spirit they are:
a. Neither able nor willing to return to God.
b. Neither able nor willing to reform the depravity of their nature.
c. Neither able nor willing to dispose themselves to reformation.

Article 16
The fall itself brought upon humanity: depravity and spiritual death, and as a result man can have no hope of being able to rise from his fall by his own free will.

Using the King James Version as our guide, it should be noted at the outset that although the word "depravity " is used by the Canons, it is not used anywhere in the Bible.

The Canons also describe human nature, inter alia, as "prone to evil." Had the Synod left it at that, they would have been in substantial agreement with Job. Unfortunately, they went far beyond that, and adopted our view, for which God reprimanded us.

In short, the Synod was of the view that all non-Christians are so depraved, so utterly dead in sin, so destitute of all powers unto spiritual good that they cannot hunger and thirst after righteousness, nor can they offer a contrite and broken spirit that is pleasing to God.[12] In support of this view, the Synod relied on the following verses.

1. Ephesians 2:1. *You are dead through your trespasses and sins.*

There are a number of factors to bear in mind as we consider this passage. The reference to death is a metaphor, and as such we must be careful not to draw out the metaphor beyond that which it intends to demonstrate.

If the word "dead" is meant to demonstrate that man is very wicked, then what is to be made of the phrase in Jude 1:12, where godless men are described as "twice dead?" If the dead are those "in trespasses and sins," then who are those that are twice dead? Is that a category reserved for people who are even worse than the trespassers and sinners?

The fact is, the Bible is full of metaphors. Christ is said to be the bread and the water, the gate, the lamb, the shepherd and the light etc. Christians are said to be sheep. The list goes on, but thin is the theology that is based on a one-word metaphor.

Jesus used the concept of death as a metaphor for separation from God. For example, in the parable of the prodigal son the father states: "For this son of mine was dead and is alive again; he was lost and is found."[13] In the parable the word "dead" is not meant to describe the absence of good in the son's life. Rather, it simply means that for a period of time the father and son had no relationship. It is worth noting that in the parable, the son returned of his own volition with a contrite and broken spirit. However, the Canons teach, that the son could not have returned, because in their natural state, man has no desire to return to God.

In John 5, Jesus declares: "whoever hears my word and believes him who sent me, has eternal life and will not be condemned; he has crossed over from death to life. I tell you the truth, a time is coming and has now come when the dead will hear the voice of the Son of God, and those who hear will live."[14] Clearly, those separated from God have the capacity to hear His voice, and if they believe, they will cross over from death to life; i.e. from separation to reunion. This passage is completely contrary to the message of the Canons, which teaches that people are so spiritually dead they have no capacity to respond to the Gospel.

To use the word "dead" as the Canons do was obviously not Paul's intent. Paul was not trying to describe the degree of wickedness of the unregenerate, but rather, to express that their relationship with God is nonexistent. In Ephesians 5, he quotes with approval an unknown source; "Wake up, O sleeper, rise from the dead, and Christ will shine on you."[15] Paul is calling the unbeliever to respond spiritually, in circumstances where the Canons teach no such response is possible.

2. Genesis 6:5. Just before the flood, *"God saw that the wickedness of man was great in the earth, and that every imagination of the thoughts of the heart were evil continually."*

The Canons use this passage in support of the proposition that <u>all</u> non-Christians are depraved, dead in sin, destitute of all spiritual good, etc. However, this passage says nothing of the sort. It simply describes the level of wickedness of a certain group, at a certain time, as: "great." But even at that time, not all people were equally wicked. In fact, some were not wicked at all. A few verses later we read; "but Noah found favor in the eyes of the Lord. He was a righteous man, blameless among the people of his time, and he walked with God."[16] The passage then talks about his sons, at least two of who were also righteous. It describes the general characteristics of a group of people, but it does not describe, nor does it intend to describe, the character of each person within that group.

2. <u>Regarding the natural and civil aspect</u>:

The Synod of Dort admitted, that even though unbelieving people are spiritually dead, they do retain some glimmerings of natural light. Natural light is described in Chapters III and IV, Articles 4 and 16.

Article 4
    A. Since the fall there remains in people glimmerings of natural light so that they retain:
        1. Some knowledge of God, and of natural things.

2. Some knowledge of the difference between good and evil.
   3. Some regard for virtue, and for good outward behavior.
B. But this light of nature:
   1. Is insufficient to bring a person to a saving knowledge of God.
   2. Is insufficient to bring a person to a true conversion.
C. Further, this light of nature (such as it is):
   1. People are incapable of using it properly even in things natural and civil.
   2. People in various ways render wholly polluted and
   3. People hinder, by doing what is inexcusable before God.

Article 16
A. The fall did not cause people:
   1. To be devoid of understanding and will, nor
   2. To deprive them of human nature, but it did bring depravity and spiritual death.

What this means is that an unbeliever is incapable of using knowledge or virtue properly "even in things natural and civil," and in various ways renders them "wholly polluted." Further, they "hinder" the natural light "in unrighteousness," by doing what "is inexcusable before God." Simply put, whatever good exists is, by a non-Christian, converted to evil. This begs the question, what is left of the natural light, if what the Canons say is true?

It is beyond dispute that non-Christians exemplify compassion, consideration, love, loyalty, fidelity, faithfulness, generosity, gentleness, honesty, humility, etc. To describe either their virtues, or their good behavior, as wholly polluted glimmerings that they cannot use aright even in things natural or civil is to deny reality. To suggest otherwise, is to make the same mistake my friends and I made, when we refused to accept the evidence of good, in favor of our religious beliefs.

Even the Synod of Dort had to acknowledge that some non-Christians behave well. However, this could not very well be described as "good behavior" because, according to the Canons, non-Christians are "unwilling to reform the depravity of their nature, (and) do what is inexcusable before God." As a result the Synod describes this behavior as, "good <u>outward</u> behavior" which suggest that the behavior was motivated for selfish reasons.

The Synod of Dort relied on the following two verses in opposition to the proposition, "that the will of itself is able to ... choose, or not to ... choose, all manner of good that may be presented to it."[17]

1. Jeremiah 17:9. *"The heart is deceitful above all things, and desperately wicked:* who can know it?"

There is no doubt that people can be deceitful and desperately wicked. But is it true that all people are totally depraved? In my view, verse 9 must be read with verse 10, which states; "I the Lord search the heart and examine the mind to reward a man according to his conduct." What is there to reward if a person is incapable of any good?

2. Ephesians 2:3. *"Among whom (sons of disobedience) we also all once lived in the lusts of our flesh, doing the desires of the flesh and of the mind.*

The Synod takes the view that Paul is describing all non-Christians as those who live in the lusts of the flesh. They are so depraved that they are unable to will, or choose to do otherwise.

There are some commentators that believe the phrase "lusts of the flesh" refers to sexual sins. If that were true, then Paul is saying that all non-Christians live their lives in pursuit of sexual gratification. That is transparently and indisputably, absurd. In law, judges will seek to avoid an interpretation that leads to an absurdity.

I agree with the Cambridge Bible. "The word 'Lusts' is narrowed in modern usage to a special class of sensual appetites, but the older English knew no such fixed restriction; Sinful 'lusts' are thus all desires, whether gross or fine in themselves, which are against the will of God."[18] What Paul means, is that because all non-Christians are alienated from God, they do what is in their self-interest to do. However, that does not mean that they are unable to choose to do any good.

Even if it were true that all non-Christians live their lives in pursuit of sexual gratification, that does not, of itself, mean that they could not choose to live differently. Because people choose poorly, does not mean that they were compelled to do so.

D. Conclusion

Augustine taught that in the absence of the regenerating power of the Holy Spirit, human nature is willingly depraved, corrupt, and enslaved to sin. Calvin depicts the human nature of the unsaved as: accursed, defiled, polluted, depraved, degenerate, corrupt, odious, abominable, and a seedbed of sin. De Bres describes the unregenerate, i.e. the non-Christian as: wicked, perverse, corrupt, vile, and enslaved to sin. The Synod of Dort characterizes the nature of the unsaved as: depraved, blind, vane, perverse, wicked, vicious, rebellious, obstinate, impure, corrupt, disobedient, prone to evil, in bondage to sin and incapable of natural or civil good.

I am not sure why Augustine, Calvin, de Bres and the Synod of Dort felt compelled to go to such extremes, especially given that they had the benefit of our debate and the entire Scriptures. Having experienced God's anger, because of our disparaging description of the Crown of His creation, I wonder what He would say to them.

Almost all Christians, including the leaders of the early church, agree that through the fall of Adam and Eve, people acquired a sinful nature. The issue is not whether all non-Christian are accursed, defiled, polluted, depraved, degenerate, corrupt, odious, abominable and a seedbed of sin (to use the words of Calvin). The real issue is this: is it necessary for all human beings, however good or evil, to be reconciled with God?

CHAPTER 10

THE SCRIPTURAL VIEW OF HUMAN NATURE

After the debate, God strongly disapproved of our concept of human nature – now carried forward by the Canons of Dort. However, our debate was not the only book in Scripture to consider this concept. It is also repudiated elsewhere.

1. The Creation and fall of Adam and Eve

The Bible chronicles the creation of man as follows: "Then God said, 'Let us make man in our own image, in our likeness, and let them have dominion over the earth.' And God did so, and He saw all that He had made, and it was very good."[1] In Proverbs, wisdom is personified. When God created the world, "I (wisdom) was the craftsman at God's side. I was filled with delight day after day, rejoicing always in His presence, rejoicing in His whole world and delighting in mankind."[2]

But Adam and Eve sinned, and God banished them from the Garden of Eden. The nature of their sin and their banishment are recorded in Genesis 3.

2. The Effect of the fall

The apostle Paul describes the effects of Adam's sin as follows, "Therefore, just as sin entered the world through one man, and death through sin, and in this way death came to all men, because all have sinned...."[3]

We have already seen how both the Confession and the Canons describe the extent of the sinfulness of human nature. In short, they allege that the whole of human nature is wicked, perverse and corrupt in all his ways. Moreover, the corruption of the whole nature is a hereditary disease, wherewith infants are already infected in their mothers womb.

Job strenuously objected to this characterization of human nature. When addressing God, whom he describes as "the Preserver of Men", he inquires: "What is man that you make so much of him, that you give him so much attention?"[4] His answer is personal. It is because: "your hands shaped me and made me ... you molded me like clay ... you clothed me with skin and flesh and knit me together with bones and sinews ... you gave me life and showed me kindness, and in your providence watched over my spirit.... In your hand is the life of every creature and the breath of all mankind.... You will call and I will answer you; you will long for the creature your hands have made."[5] In his final speech, he relates how he was always respectful of everyone because: "God created both me and my servants. He created us both in the womb."[6]

King David also describes God's regard for man, as he now is: "What is man that you are mindful of him, or the son of man that you care for him? You made him a little lower than the heavenly beings, and crowned him with glory and honor."[7] He then relates how God's esteem for humanity, is manifest in him as well. "You created my inmost being; you knit me together in my mother's womb. I praise you because I am fearfully and wonderfully made; your works are wonderful, I know that full well."[8]

In Isaiah, God identifies himself as the one "who spread out the earth and all that comes out of it, who gives breath to its people, and life to those who walk on it." A few chapters later the prophet reminds the Israelites that it was God "who made you and formed you."[9] Similarly, in Zechariah, God identifies Himself as "the Lord, who stretches out the heavens, who lays the foundation of the earth, and who forms the spirit of man within him."[10]

After our debate, God affirms that it was He, "who endowed the heart with wisdom and gave understanding to the mind."[11] Similarly, Proverbs declares that it is God who gives wisdom, knowledge, understanding, discretion and sound judgment.[12] To say that these God-given gifts are mere glimmerings, is an affront to God. Although some people are gifted more than others, the Biblical truth, and the reality is; all people enjoy these gifts in various degrees. The fall did not re-create us into something that we were not before. Men did not become maggots, nor did women become worms.

Paul compares what we now are, to what we will be, when full fellowship with God is restored: "Now we see but a poor reflection as in a mirror; then we shall see face to face. Now I know in part; then I shall know fully...."[13] As Adam's offspring, and the carriers of the image of God: we may not see clearly, but we still see; we may not know fully, we still know in part; we may not understand everything, but we still understand something.

It did not escape our attention, that when God spoke to Job, He did not address him as a maggot or a worm. Rather, on at least three occasions God addressed him as follows, "Brace yourself like a man; I will question you, and you will answer me."[14] Clearly God addressed Job as a person of understanding, capable of giving a voluntary and positive response.

After the fall, the heart of man did not become the heart of the devil. Had that been the case the battle would be over, and Satan the victor. Human nature is influenced by both good and evil, but it remains human nature. Good people are not born gods, and bad people are not born devils. The heart and mind of man remains the arena in which the battle is fought, and is subject to the influences of the war within. As such, men are capable of great evil, but they are also capable of great good. Some choose to become serial killers, while others such as Job, choose otherwise.

What Bildad, Zophar, and I should have asked: "if what we said were true, where does that put people, all of whom God fashioned, and crowned with glory and honor? What is humanity's place in the universe? Are men and women the managers of God's wonderful creation of which they are also a part, or are they the equivalent to maggots or worms, enslaved to sin?" My friends and I now understand, that if human nature is as we described, then not only did we taint His creation with corruption, but the crown of His creation "wastes away like something rotten, like a garment eaten by moths."[15]

3. Free will

At various times during the debate we said that for all people, evil is sweet and they cannot let it go; they crave evil and have no respite from their cravings. I categorically stated, that all those born of a woman are so evil, that there is an absolute certainty that they would sin. They cannot choose otherwise, because they were born with an evil nature. Job could not be righteous, because he, like all mortals, had no capacity to be so. He could not choose to be upright in character, when his nature is corrupt. Neither could he choose to be blameless in conduct, when his nature is to do wrong.

Unfortunately, some churches now teach, what my friends and I espoused at the time of the debate, and which earned us God's rebuke. The Canons state, that in the absence of the regenerating spirit, the "will" of all people is dead, evil, disobedient and refractory, and therefore, people are "neither able nor willing to ... reform the depravity of their nature." Hence, "man can have no hope of being able to rise from his fall by his own free will."[16]

It is not that people have no will: it is that, in their natural state, every person's will is programmed to choose against the good, and in favor of evil. They cannot help themselves, because, according to the Canons, they are not only prone to evil, but in bondage thereto. In other words, although they have a will, their will is not free. We used different wording, but the gist was the same. We said that all people crave evil, and have no respite from their cravings.

I now realize that what we said, and what the Canons teach, is completely contrary to Scripture. Free will is the freedom to choose between alternatives. I believe that everyone understands; if people do not have a free will, then preaching and missions would be useless, and the Great Commission and the Final Judgment a sham.

It is true that nowhere in the Bible does it explicitly state that people have a free will, probably because the Biblical writers thought it was self-evident. Consequently, it must be inferred. The following passages and verses demonstrate that the inference is inescapable.

Genesis 2:15-17 The Lord took Adam, and put him in the Garden of Eden to work in it, and to take care of it. And the Lord commanded, "<u>you are free</u> to eat from any tree in the garden; but you <u>must not</u> eat from the tree of the knowledge of good and evil, for when you eat of it you will surely die." Despite the fact that Adam and Eve were "very good", and despite God's express command, the couple <u>chose</u> to disobey God and eat of the tree. The question then becomes: was "free will" lost as a result of the fall?

Genesis 4:3-8 This passage contains the story of Cain and Abel. The problem began when both Cain and Abel brought their offerings to God. But Cain short-changed God, and as a result God did not look with favor on his offering, which caused Cain to become angry. Then the Lord said to Cain: "why are you angry? <u>If</u> you do what is right, will you not be accepted?" But Cain chose not to do what was right, and he eventually killed his brother Abel.

Deuteronomy 30:19,20 Shortly before entering the promised land, Moses announces: "This day I call heaven and earth as witnesses against you, that I have set before you life and death, blessings and curses. Now <u>choose</u> life, so that your children may live."

Joshua 24:15,22 Unfortunately, the Israelites did not always choose wisely, and God renews his challenge to them, except this time through Joshua. Again they were given a choice. "But <u>if</u> serving the Lord seems undesirable to you, then choose for yourselves this day whom you will serve." After the people assured Joshua that they would serve the Lord, Joshua confirms their promise: "you are witnesses against yourselves that you have chosen to serve the Lord." Despite their promises, many people again chose otherwise.

In a similar vein, all of the following passages demonstrate that people are able to respond of their own volition.

1 Kings 18:21 "Elijah went before the people and said, 'How long will you waver between two opinions? If the Lord is God, follow Him; but if Baal is God, follow him.'" Obviously, the choice that Elijah was offering was intended to be a real choice. But if what we, and the Canons said were true, then Elijah's words were a pretense, because the people were in bondage to sin, and therefore, could only choose Baal.

Isaiah 1:19 "If you are willing and obedient, you will eat the best from the land: but if you resist and rebel, you will be devoured by the sword." What possible meaning can be given to the phrase "if you are willing," if man does not have a free will?

Revelations 22:17 "Whoever is thirsty, let him come; and whoever wishes, let him take the free gift of the water of life." The phrase "whoever wishes" can have no meaning if what we said was true.

Luke 13:34 "I have longed to gather your children together, as a hen gathers her chicks under her wings, but you were not willing." Jesus is obviously speaking of the Jews who had exercised their free will to their detriment.

John 5:39,40 "These are the Scriptures that testify about me, yet you refuse to come to me."

The word "if" in all the following passages suggests that the happening of certain events is conditional on the choices that people make.

Matthew 16:24 "Then Jesus said to his disciples, If anyone would come after me, he must deny himself and take up his cross and follow me." This same massage is repeated in **Mark 8:34**, and in **Luke 9:23**.

John 8:24 "I told you that you would die in your sins; <u>if</u> you do not believe that I am the one I claim to be."

John 11:40 "Then Jesus said, did I not tell you that <u>if</u> you believed, you would see the glory of God."

Romans 4:24 Righteousness shall be imputed to us "<u>if</u> we believe on him that raised up Jesus our Lord from the dead." (KJV)

Romans 10:9, 10 "<u>If</u> you confess with your mouth, Jesus is Lord, and believe in your heart that God raised Him from the dead, you will be saved. For it is with your heart that you believe and are justified...."

1 Thess. 4:14 "<u>If</u> we believe that Jesus died and rose again, even so those who died in Christ, will God bring with Him."

Hebrews 10:26,27 "<u>If</u> we <u>deliberately</u> keep on sinning after we have received the knowledge of the truth, no sacrifice for sins is left, but only a fearful expectation of judgment."

1 John 1:9 "<u>If</u> we confess our sins, He is faithful and just and will forgive us our sins...."

It should be obvious to anyone that the word "if" in the above passages means that we do have a choice. We can choose to believe, to repent, to confess, to follow, to obey, or not.

Contrary to what I once believed, it is not a certainty that all people will choose to do evil. I now know that each day affords us the opportunity to choose for good, and to manage His creation accordingly.

To say of all people, that evil is sweet and they cannot let it go; that they crave evil and have no respite from their cravings; that they are prone to evil and in bondage to sin: is to say that they cannot choose for God. If that choice is denied them, then preaching, and especially missionary work, becomes a waste of time.

The notion that people do not have a free will was completely rejected by the early Church. In her book, Professor Pagels notes: "Orthodox Christians of the second and third centuries, from Justin and Irenaeus through Tertullian, Clement, and the brilliant teacher Origen, stood unanimously against the Gnostics in proclaiming the Christian gospel as a message of freedom—moral freedom, freedom of the will...." They believed that free will was "humanity's essential, God-given attribute."[17]

John Calvin acknowledges that the early church extolled the concept of a free will, but suggests that no certainty can be obtained from their writings. Specifically he states: "Although the Greek Fathers, above others, and especially Chrysostom, have exceeded due bounds in extolling the powers of the human will, yet ancient theologians, with the exception of Augustine, are so confused, vacillating, and contradictory on the subject, that no certainty can be obtained from their writings."[18]

Mako A. Nagasawa is the founder and director of the New Humanity Institute. In a book entitled: *Human Free Will and God's Grace in the Early Church Fathers*, he disagrees with Calvin's conclusion that no certainty could be obtained from the early theologians.[19] He then quotes from two prominent church historians, Philip Schaff and J.N.D. Kelly, to prove his point.[20] Schaff writes: "The Greek ... fathers ... laid great stress upon human freedom, and upon the indispensible cooperation of the freedom with divine grace."[21] Kelly agrees: "A point on which they ... were all agreed was that man's will remains free; we are responsible for our acts."[22] One of the reasons that the early church fathers stressed free will was that without it, there could be no human responsibility.

In his, *Oration On The Dignity Of Man*, Pico Della (a philosopher) writes: "Imagine! The great generosity of God! The happiness of man! To man it is allowed to be whatever he chooses to be! As soon as an animal is born, it brings out of its mother's womb all that it will ever possess. Man, when he entered life, the Father gave the seeds of every kind and every way of life possible. Whatever seeds each man sows and cultivates will grow and bear him proper fruit. ... Man is multitudinous, varied, and ever changing. Why do I emphasize this? Considering that we are born with this condition, that is, that we can become whatever we choose to become, we need to understand that we must take earnest care about this.... Above all, we should not make that freedom of choice God gave us into something harmful, for it was intended to be for our advantage. Let a holy ambition enter into our souls; let us not be content with mediocrity, but strive after the highest and expend all our strength in achieving it."[23] The Oration was written and published in 1485, 50 years before Calvin's Institutes.

4. Righteousness and regeneration

Why did Job consider himself righteous? His answer: "God knows the way that I take: and when He has tested me, I will come out as gold. My feet have closely followed His steps; I have kept to his way without turning aside, I have not departed from the commands of His lips: I have treasured the words of His mouth."[24]

King David had the same view of righteousness. In Psalm 18 he states: "The Lord has dealt with me according to my righteousness; according to the cleanness of my hands he has rewarded me. For I have kept the ways of the Lord; I have not done evil by turning from my God. All his laws are before me. I have not turned away from his decrees. I have been blameless before him and have kept myself from sin."[25]

What then are we to make of Paul's declaration in Romans 3? "There is no one righteous, not even one...."[26]

The reason for the disparity is that the word "righteous" has a different meaning in the Old and the New Testament. In the Old Testament it refers to those who were obedient. They are described as "those who did not sin by breaking a command."[27]

In the New it refers to those who were redeemed. This is clear from the words of Paul. "The righteousness that is of the law: the man who does those things shall live by them. But the righteousness that is of faith says: ... that if you confess with your mouth that Jesus is Lord, and believe in your heart that God raised him from the dead, you will be saved. For it is with the heart that that you believe unto righteousness; and with the mouth confession is made unto salvation."[28]

As a result, in the New Testament, the thief on the cross to whom Christ said, "Today you will be with me in paradise," would be considered righteous, even though his life had been one of disobedience. On the other hand the rich young ruler who had kept all the commandments since he was a boy, would be considered unrighteous, even though his life had been one of obedience.[29] Hence if someone were to ask whether only the regenerate could be righteous, the answer is, "yes," because they are defined as such.

5. Obedience

Bearing in mind that at the time of our debate the word righteous meant obedience, the question then becomes: was Job obedient because of something God did for him, or did his obedience arise out of his own free will?

When God first met Satan, He described Job as a man of blameless conduct and an upright character, who fears God and shuns evil. Satan's response was: of course that is true, but that is because you have protected him and caused him to prosper. However, if you take away your protection and deprive him of everything he has then he will curse you. So God gave Satan control over everything that Job had including his family and all his possessions.

Notwithstanding Satan's best efforts, Job did not curse God, even though he believed that God was responsible for his catastrophic loss. As a result, when God speaks to Satan the second time, He points out that Job continues to be a man of blameless conduct and upright character, who fears God and shuns evil. He further reminds Satan that Job had, "maintained his integrity even though you incited me against him to ruin him without reason."[30]

If there were ever a circumstance where it would be difficult to be obedient it was the circumstance in which Job found himself. The benefit of God's protection was removed when Satan took control of his life. Even my friends and I urged him to do what he knew to be untrue, i.e. to deny that he was righteous. Throughout his suffering, he remained honest and consistent to his beliefs, and he chose not to give that up.

So what was it that caused Job to remain steadfast and to maintain his integrity? Obviously God was not protecting or assisting him. Job stood alone before the power of the devil. He maintained his integrity and remained obedient because he chose to do so.

6. Obedience and regeneration.

This brings us to the next question. Is obedience by itself sufficient to be reconciled with God? The answer is, "no," but why not?

Every person, including the obedient has a propensity to sin. Therefore, it is not possible for an obedient person to be reconciled with the very God that he has a propensity to sin against.

I do not want to judge Job as I once did, but his own words indicate that he knew that during the debate he might have yielded to the propensity to sin. He had challenged God, and God had corrected him. In reaction to the correction Job confessed, "I repent in dust and ashes." If Job did not think that he had sinned, then what was he repenting of?

To be obedient does not mean that one is perfect, From Hebrews we learn that someday all people, including "the spirits of the righteous men made perfect," will come before God the judge of all men. (The authorship of "Hebrews" is not known, but whoever it was is using the word "righteous" in the Old Testament sense.) What this means, is that even the obedient must be redeemed, i.e., made perfect by "Jesus the mediator of a new covenant," and by His "sprinkled blood."[31]

According to the writer of Hebrews, the new covenant has retroactive application, even to those in the Old Testament who were considered righteous i.e., obedient – like my friend Job, or my grandfather Abraham. The Apostle James, asks the following rhetorical question: "Was not our ancestor Abraham considered righteous for what he did when he offered his son Isaac on the alter?"[32] The answer of course is "yes." But that was not the type of righteousness that was sufficient to save. In Hebrews, the writer argues that Abraham's ultimate redemption was not an act of obedience, but an act of faith when he writes: "By faith Abraham ... offered Isaac as a sacrifice."[33]

7. The non-Christian person

The Canons describe those who have not received the regenerating grace of the Holy Spirit as "the unregenerate man." These are the people, who, notwithstanding their total depravity, did retain,
1. Some knowledge of God;
2. Some knowledge of natural things;
3. Some knowledge of the difference between good and evil;
4. Some regard for virtue; and
5. Some regard for good outward behavior.

The Canons refer to items 1 – 5 above, as glimmerings of natural light. It alleges that the unregenerate man (i.e. a non-Christian or an unbeliever) is incapable of using these glimmerings properly "even in things natural and civil," and in various ways renders them "wholly polluted." Further, the non-

Christian "hinders" the natural light "in unrighteousness," by doing what "is inexcusable before God."[34]

But is the forgoing what the Bible teaches? *The Book of Proverbs* (Proverbs) is a book of general application. That is, it is intended for the daily benefit of all people. In Chapter 1, King Solomon sets out the purposes for recording his proverbs. They are:

1. For attaining wisdom and discipline,
2. For acquiring a disciplined and prudent life,
3. For doing what is right and just and fair,
4. For giving prudence to the simple, and
5. For giving knowledge and discretion to the young.[35]

All of the proverbs are intended to impart some knowledge of God; some knowledge of the difference between good and evil; and some regard for virtue. Consequently, they all fall within the Canons' definition of "natural light." Nonetheless, the Canons proclaim that an unbelieving person "wholly pollutes" such knowledge, by using it to do what is indefensible before God. In so doing they have rendered the proverbs useless for anyone other than Christians.

For example, in Proverbs, King Solomon urges his son to listen to your father's instruction, and do not forsake your mother's teaching.[36] What evidence is there, that a non-Christian person would, or even could, use this good advice improperly? Why would a mother teach her unbelieving son anything, if such teachings were rendered wholly polluted because her son used it to do what was unforgivable? Also in Proverbs, Solomon instructs: "if sinners entice you, do not give in to them."[37] Clearly this verse is importing some knowledge of good and evil and hence qualifies as a glimmering of natural light. But under what circumstance could this advice be used inappropriately?

By stretching the doctrine of total depravity as far as they did, the Synod of Dort effectively pulled it into the realm of the absurd. I have no intention of going through all the proverbs, but I challenge the reader to find one that unbelieving persons could render wholly polluted because they used it improperly.

Throughout the Book of Proverbs, all people are encouraged to embrace various virtues such as: humility, integrity, faithfulness, truthfulness, goodness, fidelity, diligence, love, discernment, understanding, hopefulness, gentleness, cheerfulness, compassion, patience, joyfulness, honesty and prudence. One wonders whether Solomon would have extolled these virtues if he had known that the unchristian recipient would somehow use it "to do what is inexcusable before God."

Not only do the Proverbs promote various virtues, but they also identify people of virtuous character, which includes non-Christians. These are people who please God, and from whom others can learn.[38] Included in this list are: a kindhearted woman, a kind man, a generous man, a good man, a wife of noble character, a prudent man, a truthful witness, a discerning man, a man of knowledge and a faithful man etc. The Canons teach that an unregenerate person cannot do what is right, "even in things natural and civil." How then can they be as described in the Proverbs, i.e. kind, generous, noble etc?

In Mark, Jesus is confronted by a rich young ruler, who asks him, "what must I do to inherit eternal life?" Jesus tells him to keep the commandments, to which the young man replies: "all these I have kept since I was a boy." Jesus looked at him and loved him.[39] Can it, in any meaningful way, be said that this man's regard for virtue in keeping the commandments, was inexcusable before God?

In Luke, Jesus is heard speaking to His disciples. "If you love those who love you, what credit is that to you? Even sinners love those who love them. And if you do good to those who are good to you, what credit is that to you? Even sinners do that."[40] This passage demonstrates that the unbeliever is capable of loving and doing good. The fact that the love and good works are directed to those who respond in kind does not mean that the goodness of the unbeliever is improper, wholly polluted or of no value. Jesus is not disparaging the love or goodness of an unbeliever. Rather, He is calling believers to a higher standard. His message is: do not just love or do good when it is easy to do so, laudable as that may be. Also love and do good when it is difficult.

8. Reflections

You will recall that the debate began when Job asked the following provocative question: "Why is life given to those who have no future and whom God has hedged in with suffering?"[41] Implicit in the question is the contention that God was responsible for his suffering.

I immediately took issue with Job and attempted to prove, that because of his sinful nature, he was himself responsible, and God was merely punishing him for sins that he must have committed. My problem was that I had no evidence of any sin that Job had actually done. In fact, I knew him to be a man of pious character and blameless conduct. But I also knew that he was human, or to use another word "mortal." I fervently believed that all mortals are inherently evil, and that the evil within would manifest itself in evil deeds.

The question then is: when I look back, what should I have done differently? Not surprisingly, I have spent a great deal of time considering this question, and I have concluded that there are two things I would change. The first is my response to Job, and the second is my theology.

a. Regarding my response to Job:

I am consumed by remorse for the pain I caused my friend. When he was already overburdened with suffering, I attempted to take away his one comfort, i.e., God's reward for his obedience. His righteousness caused him to be hopeful, and I should have affirmed what I knew to be true.

Prior to the debate we were a brotherhood of kindred souls, and we relished the solicitude of friendship. The esteem given each other nourished us. We were genuinely concerned about the welfare of the other, and we were happy for the other's successes. Our hearts harmonized, and on most issues we enjoyed complete solidarity. Our discourses were respectful.

Regretfully, that all changed during the debate. We treated him like a traitor: He asked for our understanding, but we rebuffed him; He pleaded for our fellowship, but we ignored him; He appealed to our brotherhood, but we deserted him. When he needed us the most, we spurned him. We left him isolated and forsaken.

I rationalized the severity of my words, by claiming that I was both defending the justice of God, and benefiting my friend. I believed that he had put his soul in jeopardy, and I wanted him to restore his relationship with God, before it was to late.

However, I now realize that my rationalization was nothing more than an excuse. Even if I had been prompted by such laudable intentions, my lofty motivation vanished after the first round. Thereafter, it became a winner-take-all brawl. As in all brawls, there are no rules, and I knowingly lied when I accused my friend of actual sins.[42]

Both God and Job have forgiving me, and I will never again value a religious precept over a person. I know that there are legitimate religious differences, but when a person is in need, the resolution of those differences can wait. What Job needed was to be comforted, not corrected.

It appears to me that nothing spawns animosity more quickly than religious differences. Communities are divided, families ripped apart, and friends no longer on speaking terms: but why? "Did not He who made me in the womb, also make them? Did not the same God form us both within our mothers?"[43]

b. Regarding my theology:

What would I change? Whatever else may be on that list, the number one change would be to accept reality, rather than to stubbornly try to restructure reality so as to make it conform to my theology. I no longer wish to hide behind the fact that my friends, Bildad and Zophar, did the same. Job had repeatedly and emphatically said that he was righteous. I, on the other hand, was so sure about my theology that I refused to accept, not just his word, but also my knowledge and experience of him.[44] Even though I was aware of his blameless character and good works, I wrongfully accused him of being a hypocrite, and of doing what he did for show. I saw his dreadful suffering with my theologically biased eyes, and in so doing, I willfully blinded myself to the truth, i.e., Job was indeed a righteous person. Jeremiah described me well when he said: "because of stubbornness, there are those, who have eyes but do not see, who have ears but do not hear."[45]

Furthermore, we all know good and upright people who are not Christians. They may be friends, neighbors, family members, or volunteers who work tirelessly in hospitals, nursing homes, schools and day cares. To suggest that these good, but unchristian friends and neighbors (whom the Canons say cannot exist) have a "wholly polluted" regard for virtue like love, loyalty, fidelity, faithfulness, truth or respect, is for many people pure nonsense, and makes Christianity look ridiculous.

To say that all people, whom God made to manage His creation, are now corrupted by Satan, and under his control, is to say that God was helpless to prevent the takeover, and powerless to take it back. Certainly He is not a God to whom the name "Almighty" would ever be attached. I had a reputation as wise man, and I should have known that my arguments undercut the concept of the sovereignty of God. He cannot be sovereign if the crowns of His creation are now enslaved to sin, and are therefore managing His creation in accordance with the dictates of another.

God described Job as "blameless and upright, a man who fears God and shuns evil." If Job was as God described (and obviously he was) then it cannot be true that all people are totally corrupt by nature, dead in sin and in bondage thereto, and are unwilling to reform the depravity of their nature.

It grieves me to see that there are those who are making the same mistake that I made, and for the same reasons. Just as I did, the Synod of Dort projected their theology onto reality, instead of allowing reality to speak to them. William Blake, an English poet, beautifully expresses the results of such an erroneous projection in the following poem:

This life's dim window of the soul
Distorts the heavens from pole to pole
And leads you to believe a lie
When you see with, not through the eye.

The reality is, there is much good in many people including non-Christians, and many people do good things. God's influence and attraction in this world is no less than that of the leviathan. To deny the goodness that exists, or to say that it is simply for show, is to be blinded by ones theology, and to discredit the sovereignty of God and the excellence of His creation. Is it any wonder that God was offended by what I had alleged?

In respect to my allegation that people are totally corrupt, there is perhaps no better answer than Job's retort: "if I say to corruption, 'you are my father,' and to the worm, 'you are my mother or my sister,' where then is my hope? Who can see any hope for me?"[46]

9. Conclusion

Prior to my encounter with God, I believed that in the eyes of God, I was no more significant than a maggot or worm, destined to do wrong, and unable to do otherwise. I also believed that God would watch for my sins, and unless I acknowledged and confessed my shortcomings, He would severely punish me, as He had Job. This drained the happiness from my life because it emphasized my insignificance, and caused me to focus on my sins and shortcomings. I was always waffling between evaluating the gravity of my offenses and the sufficiency of my confession. I dreaded the possibility of death because I was afraid that one of my sins may have been left unconfessed, and I would be faced with an angry God.

My encounter with God changed my perception of Him and of myself. I was relieved of the burden of guilt and shame, and the immobilizing feeling of inadequacy and insignificance. God himself had confirmed that what Job had said was true. When God created His cosmos (which included me), He looked at what He had done, and concluded that it was good. I acknowledge that I have a sinful nature, but I also recognize that His hands shaped me and made me; He molded me like clay; He clothed me with skin and flesh; He knit me together with bones and sinews, and He gave me wisdom and understanding. He set His heart upon me, and showed me kindness. In His providence He watched over my spirit. I know that, notwithstanding my sinful nature, He does not spurn the work of His hands.

I now considered myself the most fortunate person in the world. What a privilege, what a joy, to be working for the one who made me, who cares for me, who rescues me from my mistakes, and who crowns me with glory and honor.

What a priceless and undeserved gift is both my life, and the opportunity to live it – in this marvelous world that He created. How can I survey the sun, the moon, and the stars and not be in awe of Him who made them? How can I explore the mountains, the forests, the great plains, the rivers, the lakes, and the oceans, and not be overwhelmed by the knowledge, that they were all made by the same Creator as created me?

As you know, my body was laid to rest many years ago, and when it was my heart was filled, not with fear and dread, but with thankfulness and anticipation. I knew that I would soon meet the God who made me, who set His heart on me, who showed me kindness, who watched over my spirit, and "who longs for the person that His hands had made."[47]

END NOTES

Chapter 1
1. Jeremiah 49:7
2. Job 29:16 (KJV)
3. Job 15:28. Although I was ostensibly speaking of the habitations of the wicked, I was actually describing Job's dwelling, as a house which no man would inhabit, and which is "ready to become a heap" (KJV). In Job 18:15, Bildad states that, "burning sulfur will be scattered over his dwelling." Burning sulfur within a structure was the means used to disinfect it.
4. Job 19:16
5. In Job 20:20 Zophar is pretending to be speaking of the wicked. However he is actually describing Job's inclination to throw up when he states: "Surely he shall not feel quietness in his belly, he shall not save of that which he desired." (KJV) As far as his diarrhea is concerned, Job described it as follows: "My bowels boiled, and rested not." (Job 30:27. KJV)
6. Job 42:7,8
7. Job 1:6; 2:1
8. Job 1:8 and repeated in Job 2:3
9. Job 1:9-11
10. Job 2:3
11. Job 2:4,5
12. Job 2:9
13. *The Book of Job*, Google: Professor Rabbi Yitzchak Breitowitz at https://www.youtube.com/watch?v=e9LB47o4Q9M.
    (Professor Breitowitz lives in Jerusalem, but has maintained his status as a tenured professor at the Maryland School of Law.)

Chapter 2

1. *The New Oxford Annotated Bible with the Apocrypha, Expanded Edition,* ed. Herbert G. May and Bruce M. Metzger (Oxford University Press, 1977). See the footnote on p. 618.
2. Job 6:6,7. www.biblehub.com/commentaries. There is a question as to the meaning of this passage. Some believe that Job is criticizing me for my unsavory remarks. I disagree. Job's criticism of my remarks does not begin until verse 14. I agree with those who believe that Job is providing a justification for his statement that he wishes he was dead. This view is supported by the very next verse where Job declares, "I do wish that God would give me death."
3. The word devil comes from the Hebrew word "tannin," meaning an evil serpent or dragon. The ASV uses the term, "sea monster", because in our culture evil was depicted as such. See for example Isaiah 27:1.
4. Job 7:20
5. 1 Chronicles 1:32-35. Most scholars believe that the descendents of Shuah were called Shuhites, and Job 2:11 identifies Bildad as a Shuhite. My ancestry is more explicit in that my father was Esau.
6. Genesis 36:12
7. 1 Chronicles 1:36
8. Job 10:6,7
9. Job 11:11
10. Job 14:1-5
11. Job 14:15
12. Job 13:26
13. Job 12:3; 13:2
14. Job 13:12 (NLT)

Chapter 3

1. Job 15:14-16. I note that *The New International Version* (NIV) uses the word "vile." However, most translations use the word: abominable." Some use the word "detestable." Whatever the word, my meaning was clear; all people are inherently evil to their very core. See www.biblehub.com/parallel.
2. Job 15:17-30. This is another instance where I purport to be speaking of evil men generally but I obviously had Job in mind. Eventually Bildad and Zophar will follow my lead and speak to Job as if he were another person. In my summary I have done away with the pretense for all of us.
3. Job 17:14
4. Job 17:5; 17:12
5. Job 11:20
6. Job 31:16
7. Job 17:11
8. Job 14:18,19
9. Job 18:5-19. During the actual debate Bildad appears to be describing the wicked in general, when in fact he is describing what he believes to be the consequence of Job's wickedness.
10. Job 19:23-25. There are some commentaries that believe Job's reference to his "Redeemer" refers to Christ. For example, in his commentary, Matthew Henry states: "Here is much of Christ and heaven…. Job was taught by God to believe in a living Redeemer; to look for the resurrection of the dead, and the life of the world to come."

    However, the context clearly indicates that Job believed his "Redeemer who, in the end, would stand upon the earth," was God himself. In his very next sentence he affirms that although, in the end, his body may be destroyed he will see God with his own eyes.

Professor Ellicott comes to the same conclusion, albeit for different reasons. In his commentary he states that we must carefully note all the passages that lead up to this one. He then reviews Job's various descriptions of God and notes that he "had already recognized God as his judge, his umpire, his advocate, his witness and his surety." Job now recognizes God as his Redeemer, who will vindicate him.... The Pulpit Commentary shares this view for the same reasons.

The authors of the Cambridge Bible also interpret "Redeemer" to be God. They canvass the use of the word in the Old Testament and conclude: "the term Redeemer is frequently used of God as the deliverer of His people out of captivity ... and also as the deliverer of individuals from distress." See biblehub.com/commentaries

11. Job 20:22-29. Once again, during the actual debate, Zophar describes Job's punishment as if he were describing a third person.

Chapter 4
1. Job 21:14
2. Many scholars are perplexed as to the authorship and meaning of Job 24:18-25. For example, the writers of Barnes' Notes on the Bible state: "Le Clerc says that there is scarcely any passage of the scriptures more obscure than this, and the variety of rendering adopted will show at once the perplexity of expositors." The writers of the Jamieson-Fausset-Brown Commentary believe that in these verses Job quotes the opinions of his adversaries ironically. The writers of the Cambridge Bible for Schools and Colleges agree. They contend that Job 24:2-17 raises the question: What is the fate of wicked men? The answer contained in Job 24:18-21 is that of Job's friends, and is only introduced ironically and in order to supply the background to the true

picture. (The foregoing examples were all taken from biblehub.com/commentaries.)

Other commentators believe, and I agree, that Chapter 24:18-25 actually belong to Bildad. For example, The New Bible Commentary (4th ed., 1994, (Inter-Varsity Press), p 475) states: "Some of this section is so unlike Job's argument that we have to assume that it must really be the friends who are speaking here. ... Perhaps these verses were originally the missing end of Bildad's speech."

3. Although his name does not appear, Zophar's last response is recorded in Job 27:7-23. I agree with the conclusion reached by the New Bible Commentary, 2nd ed., 1965, (Eerdmans Publishing), p 402. "This passage presents a number of difficulties. The connection between Job's affirmation of innocence and the picture of the end of the wicked is hard to fathom. The friends had maintained that sinfulness was the clue to adversity, and had accordingly denied Job's innocence. That denial was the logical outcome of their creed. And now, without a trace of warning, Job appears as a perfervid believer in that creed. In the second place the passage flatly contradicts what Job had said about the prosperity of the wicked.... On the other hand, this passage would sound perfectly in place on the lips of the friends." Because of these disparities and contradictions "many scholars hold that there has been a dislocation in the book at this point, and attribute this section to Zophar, which would mean that all the friends speak three times."

Chapter 5
1. Job 3:23
2. Job 15:14-16
3. See Job 15:11 (KJV)

4. Job 11:11
5. See Proverbs 4:23 and Matthew 15:19
6. Job 20:12,13,20
7. Job 5:7
8. Job 7:17; 10:3,8-12; 14:1-5
9. Job 27:2-6
10. Job 1:5
11. Job 29:12-14
12. Job 29:7-25
13. See Job 8:4 and Job 11:6
14. The International Standard Bible Encyclopedia. Taken from the biblehub.com/lexicon
15. Job 31:2,3
16. Job 14:4
17. Job 14:1,2,5
18. Job 14:3
19. Job 7:20 (KJV)
20. Job 9:29,30
21. Job 4:7,8,12,13
22. Job 7:17,18,19; 15:2,7-10, 17-19; 22:2-5
23. Job 8:8-10; 11:5,6; 20:4,5
24. Job 1:8; 2:3
25. Job 38:36

Chapter 6
1. Job 10:3; 13:21-24
2. Job 19:6,7
3. Job 23:4,5
4. Job 38:2,3
5. Job 40:4,5
6. Job 40:2,8
7. Job 40:7
8. Job 42:1-6
9. Job's complaints are found in Job 9:7-11; 23:8,9, while God's response is found in 38:4,5,12,31-33

10. Psalm 19:1-4
11. Job 14:1
12 Genesis 3:17-19
13. Job 38:40. Most translations use the idiom "lie in wait." The writers of some commentaries believe that the idiom is descriptive of the lioness and not the cubs. I disagree. According to thefreedictionary.com "to lie in wait" can mean:
> a. To stay still and hidden, waiting for someone or something.
> b. To stay hidden ready to attack.
> c. To delay doing something until the best time for it.

https://idioms.thefreedictionary.com/lie+in+wait. I believe that the first meaning applies in this case, and is descriptive of the cubs' behavior.
14. Job 4:11
15. Psalm 104:21
16. Psalm 147:9
17. Luke 12:24
18. See Job 39:1-4
19. Job 39:1. That was why David chose to hide in these hard to reach places forcing Saul "to seek David and his men among the rocks of the wild goats." (1 Samuel 24:2)
20. Job39:3
21. Job 39:3. For example, *Webster's New World College Dictionary*, 4th edition, defines pain, inter alia, as "the labor of childbirth."
22. Psalm 29:9
23. Job 6:5
24. Job 24:5 (NLT)
25. Jeremiah 14:6
26. Job 23:13,14
27. Proverbs 30:18,19

28. *The New Oxford Annotated Bible with the Apocrypha, Expanded Edition,* ed. Herbert G. May and Bruce M. Metzger (Oxford University Press, 1977). "Evil (is) personified by the monsters Behemoth and Leviathan." p 613.
29. Job 3:8
30. Job 15:14-16; 20:12,13,20; 25:4-6
31. Isaiah 14:12
32. Psalm 74:14
33. Revelation 12:7-9,12
34. Isaiah 27:1
35. Revelation 13:1-10
36. Ephesians 6:10-12
37. Job 41:33
38. Job 40:2
39. Proverbs 16:5
40. Isaiah 14:12-14
41. Ezekiel 28:15-17
42. Genesis 3:5
43. Job 40:11,12

Chapter 7
1. Job 42:7,8
2. Job 4:7,8; 5:6,7 NLT
3. Job 15:14-16,35 NLT
4. Job 22:6-9
5. Job 8:4 NLT
6. Job 18:5-19
7. Job 25:4-6
8. Job 11:11 KJV
9. Ibid 11:10
10. Ibid 11:6
11. Job 20:12,13,20
12. Job 27:13
13. Ibid 27:14-23

14. Ezekiel 14:14
15. Hebrews 11:4,5,8
16. 1 Samuel 3:20
17. 2 Chronicles 22:9
18. 2 Kings 15:34
19. 2 Kings 18:5,6
20. 2 Kings 22:2; 23:25
21. Genesis 1:26,31
22. Proverbs 8:30
23. Job 7:17; 10:11,12
24. Job 14:15
25. Job 31:15
26. Psalm 8:4,5
27. Psalm 139:14
28. Isaiah 44:2-4; 46:3,4
29. Zechariah 12:1
30. Job 7:20
31. Isaiah 46:3,4
32. Genesis 1:28
33. Genesis 2:4-7,15
34. Isaiah 45:18
35. Psalm 8:6
36. Job 9:4-13, and 26:12,13 respectively. Instead of using the phrase "monsters of the sea", many translations, such as the New International Version, use the phrase "cohorts of Rahab." However, in a footnote, the New Living Translation explains that "Rahab" was the name of a mythical sea monster that represents chaos in ancient literature. See also Isaiah 27:1 where the monster of the sea is pictured as an evil creature along with the Leviathan.
37. Job 1:8
38. Job 17:14,15
39. Job 42:7,8
40. Job 6:10

41. Job 7:17,18
42. Job 7:20
43. Job 9:4-10
44. Job 9:29
45. Job 9:30,31
46. Job 10:2,3
47. Job 10:5-12
48. Job 10:18,19
49. Job 12:7-10
50. Job 13:4-8
51. Job 13:8-16
52. Job 13:23
53. Job 13:28
54. Job 14:14,15
55. Job 16:16-19
56. Job 17:14,15
57. Job 19:3-5
58. Job 19:25-29
59. Job 21:4-13
60. Job 21:23-26
61. Job 21:27-33
62. Job 21:34
63. Job 23:3-10
64. Job 24:1-12
65. Job 24:18-24
66. Job 27:2-6
67. Job 28:28
68. Job 29:14; 31:15
69. Job 31:2-4
70. Job 31:35-37

Chapter 8
1. Job 32:1-5
2. *The New Bible Commentary Inter-varsity Press*, 4th ed., 1994, p. 478

3. Richard R. Losch, *All the people in the Bible. An A-Z Guide to the Saints, Scoundrels and Other Characters in Scripture*, 2008, p. 102. It can be found on line at: https://books.google.ca/books?id=j9db9kGwG3MC&pg=PR4&dq=richard+losch+all+the+people+in+the+bible.
4. *The New Oxford Annotated Bible with the Apocrypha*, expanded edition, 1977, (Oxford University Press), p. 613
5. Ibid, p. 643
6. https://en.wikipedia.org/wik/Elihu_(Job)
7. Examples 1-7 were taken from biblehub.com/commentary
8. *New Bible Commentary*, 4th ed., 1994, p 484
9. Job 6:4; 7:11-16; 10:2,3,16,17; 14:18-22; 16:7-14; 23:13-16; 30:20-23.
10. *Matthew Henry's Commentary* taken from biblehub.com/ Commentary
11. *Benson's Commentary* taken from biblehub.com/Commentary
12. The Book of Job, Google: Professor Rabbi Yitchak Breitowitz at https://www.youtube.com/watch?v=e9LB47o409M. Professor Breitowitz is a Biblical scholar as well as a professor at the Maryland School of Law. He confirms that our position in this matter, (referring to my friends and I) was: the conventional view of morality as taught in the Pentateuch.
13. Leviticus 26:1-13
14. Deuteronomy 28:1-14
15. Vss. 3,4; 14-16, 18; 21,22; 23.24; 27,28
16. Deuteronomy 28:15-68
17. Isaiah 13:11
18. Isaiah 14:24
19. Jeremiah 44:9

20. Numbers 23:19
21. Zephaniah 1:12
22. Deuteronomy 28:63
23. Job 9:22,23; 10:3; 12:6
24. Job 14:19
25. Job 21:7-9,13

Chapter 9
1. Professor Elaine Pagels, *ADAM, EVE, and the SERPENT*, 1st ed., 1989, (Vintage Books) p. 107
2. Ibid, pp. 129,130
3. Ibid, p 99
4. Ibid. P XIX
5. St. Augustine, *City of God*, Book 13, Chapter 14, p. 10, trans by Marcus Dodds and published in 1913. Originally translated by John Healey and published in 1610. The website is: https://archive.org/details/cityofgodtransla02auguuoft
6. *ADAM, EVE and the SERPENT*, p 109
7. The information in respect to Calvin's life was extracted from *The World Book Encyclopedia*, Vol. 3 1976, and from https://en.wikipedia.org/wiki/john_calvin, and from the *Encyclopedia Britannica*, at: https://www.britannica.com/biography/Michael-Servetus.
8. All of the information for this section was taken from the Christian Classics Ethereal Library located at https://www.ccel.org.
9. The information in respect to de Bres' life was extracted primarily from Rev. W. Peter Gadsby, *Guido De Bres and the Birth of the Belgic Confession*, The Banner, 1976, and https://en.wikipedia.org/wiki/Guido_de_Bres
10. *Confession of Faith*, by Guido de Bres, Articles XIV, XV
11. The information regarding the formation of the Canons of Dort was taken from a number of sources including:

a) Canons of Dort | Theopedia found at https://www.theopedia.com/Canons_of_Dort 2. Canons of Dort/
b) Canons of Dort | Christian Reformed Church found at https://www.crcna.org/wecome/beliefs/confessions/canons-dort
c) S. Vandergugten, *The Arminian Controversy and the Synod of Dort*, found at spindleworks.com/library/vandergugten/arminian.c.htm. d) Synod of Dort | Netherlands church assembly | Britannica.com and found at https://www.britannica.com/Synod of Dort.

12. *Canons of Dort*, Chapter III-IV, paragraph 4
13. Luke 15:24
14. John 5:24,25
15. Ephesians 5:14
16. Genesis 6:8,9
17. See the Canons of Dort, Chapter III-IV, paragraph 3
18. *The Cambridge Bible for Schools and Colleges*, taken from biblehub.com

Chapter 10

1. Genesis 1:26,31
2. Proverbs 8:30
3. Romans 5:2
4. Job 7:17,20
5. Job 10:11,12; 12:10; 14:15
6. Job 31:15
7. Psalm 8:4,5
8. Psalm 139:14
9. Isaiah 42:5; 44:2,24
10. Zechariah 12:1
11. Job 38:36
12. Proverbs 2:4-6; 3:21

13. 1 Corinthians 13:12
14. Job 38:3; 40:2,7
15. Job 13:28
16. *Canons of Dort*, Chapter III-IV, Articles 3,11, 16
17. *ADAM, EVE and the SERPENT*, Vintage Books, 1st ed., 1989; pp. 73,76.
18. John Calvin, *Institutes of the Christian Religion*, Book 2, chapter 2, section 4.
19. https://blogs.ancientfaith.com/orthodoxbridge/wp-content/uploads/sites/27/2013/11/Mako-Nagasawa-free-will-in-patristics.pdf
20. Ibid
21. Ibid
22. Ibid
23. Pico Della, *Oration On The Dignity Of Man*, 1486, translated by Richard Hooker
24. Job 23:10-12
25. Psalm 18:20-23
26. Romans 3:10
27. Romans 5:14
28. Romans 5:19
29. See Luke 23: 32-43 and Mark 19:16-22
30. Job 2:3
31. Hebrews 12:23
32. James 2:21
33. Hebrews 11:17
34. Canons, Chap. III-IV, Art. 4
35. Proverbs 1:2-4
36. Proverbs 1:8
37. Proverbs 1:10
38. See Proverbs 3:4; 11:20; 12:2,22; 14:31; 15:9
39. Mark 10:17-27
40. Luke 6:32,33
41. Job 3:23
42. Job 22:5-9

43. Job 31:15
44. The writers of the New Bible Commentary, 21st Century Edition, 1994, agree. They conclude: "where they fail Job is that they take their cue from their doctrine instead of from the evidence of their eyes and ears. They know that Job is a good man, and they wrong him by thinking that his suffering is a witness against his goodness." P.460
45. Jeremiah 5:21-23
46. Job 17:14,15
47. Job 14:15

A Note to the Reader

In 2015, I began to write this book. It was my mission to make known, in whatever forum possible, the message from the Book of Job. It is a message that affirms the reality of a free will, and the potential dignity of all people – whom the Bible describes as having been "crowned with glory and honor." (Psalm 8:5) It flatly rejects the notion that all people are totally depraved, and their volition is enslaved to sin.

If you believe that the message of Job is worth disseminating, then I would like to form a partnership with you. Hopefully we can cooperate in advancing the message in whatever way we believe will be effective. I can be contacted through my website: www.winsonelgersma.com. I believe that together we can make a difference.

About the Author

I was born and raised in Neerlandia, Alberta, a small Christian community approximately seventy miles northwest of Edmonton. After graduating from high school I lived and worked for one winter in an isolated lumber camp located many miles in the bush. It was during that time that I decided to become a minister in the Christian Reformed Church (CRC). In 1967 I obtained my Bachelor of Arts degree from Dordt College in Sioux Center, Iowa; and in 1970 I earned my Bachelor of Divinity degree from Calvin Theological Seminary in Grand Rapids, Michigan. Thereafter, I became the pastor of a small Christian Reformed Church in Ackley, Iowa where my wife and I served for three years. We had three children at the time.

When I entered the ministry I was surprised to learn that I was required to sign a Form of Subscription that compelled me to defend and promote the doctrine of election as taught in the Belgic Confession (Confession), written in 1561; and the Canons of Dort (Canons), written in 1618 –19. The form provided that those who sign it *"declare by this our subscription that we heartily believe and are persuaded that all the articles and points of doctrine contained in the Confession (and the Canons) do fully agree with the word of God. We promise therefore to teach and faithfully defend the aforesaid doctrine, without either directly or indirectly contradicting the same by our public preaching or teaching."*

Over time my concerns, misgivings and doubts increased as to the biblical nature of the doctrine of election. Eventually, while studying the Book of Job, I found that in good conscience I could no longer defend this doctrine as required, and we left the ministry.

Thereafter we moved to Edmonton where I enrolled at the University of Alberta Law School. After graduating I became a trial lawyer. In 2004 I retired from my legal practice and as such I had time to think again about the doctrine of election and my reasons for leaving the ministry.

This book is about the Book of Job and its application to one of the doctrines that make up the doctrine of election, namely the total depravity of human nature. Although the doctrine of total depravity is only one of the doctrines that make up the larger doctrine of election, it is by far the most important.

www.ingramcontent.com/pod-product-compliance
Lightning Source LLC
Chambersburg PA
CBHW052030070526
44584CB00016B/1979